Teaching Multilevel Classes in ESL

Jill Bell

Dominie Press, Inc.

To my parents
Ron and Ena Sinclair
            —Jill Sinclair Bell

The following publishers have generously given permission to use quotations from copyrighted works: From *SB/LB Resource Manual*, by P. Price and S. Montgomery. Copyright 1985 by Alberta Vocational Centre, Edmonton, Alberta, Canada. Reprinted by permission of the publisher. From *How's It Going?* by Martin Good and John Holmes. Copyright 1982 by Adult Literacy & Basic Skills Unit, London, England. Reprinted by permission of the publisher. From *Teacher's Guide to Abracadabra*, by Sharon Basman. Copyright 1985 by the Board of Education for the City of North York, Ontario. Reprinted by permission of the author.

Dominie Press, Inc.
5945 Pacific Center Boulevard
San Diego, California 92121 USA

ISBN 1-56270-032-4

Printed in the United States of America

4 5 6 7 8 9 10 11 W 98 97 96 95 94 93 92

Contents

iii

88345

Acknowledgments

This book was developed in the Modern Language Centre of the Ontario Institute for Studies in Education. The project was funded through the Ontario Ministry of Education transfer grants to OISE.

I am grateful to my colleagues Marjatta Holt and Barbara Burnaby, who contributed many useful ideas, and to the following people, who kindly reviewed the manuscript and in other ways contributed ideas and materials to the book: Judith Bernstein, Brenda Duncombe, Tara Goldstein, Jean Handscombe, John Holt, Anna Hemmendinger, Fatima Pascoa, Sidney Pratt, Joan Speares, and Kathleen Troy. For their constant support and encouragement I would like to thank my husband Bob and my daughters Thalia, Kirsten, and Karen.

I would particularly like to express my gratitude to the students in the adult ESL class at C.J. Webster P.S., who so patiently tried out every activity in this book, and to their teacher, Sharon Miller, who allowed me unlimited access to her classroom as well as reviewed the manuscript.

Many of the ideas included in this book are already in widespread use or were suggested by a number of people, so that it is not always possible to credit any particular person. I am greatly indebted to many people for their help and apologize to anyone whose contribution has inadvertently not been acknowledged here. Any errors or omissions in the text are the fault of the author and not of those who so generously gave me their time and their ideas.

Introduction

Some years ago, when I was just beginning as an ESL teacher, I was offered a temporary job teaching a summer course at a suburban campus of the local university. I was very nervous, as my experience at that point was confined to community classes, and I wasn't sure what to expect in the university setting. ESL had never been offered at that campus before, so no one else around really knew what to expect either. The course had been widely advertised on campus and also in the local community press, and hopes were high that enough people would register to make the course go. Meanwhile I had been asked to name my chosen text so that the university bookstore could get sufficient copies in stock. Given my minimal experience, this request threw me into somewhat of a panic, and I spent many hours frantically reviewing texts, trying to choose the "right one," when I really didn't know whom I was supposed to be choosing for.

When I finally walked into class that first evening, all my fears were realized. The first student I took details from was an Arabic postgraduate engineering student. Sitting next to him was a middle-aged Italian couple whose only connection with the university was that they lived on the next block. The husband, a construction worker, just managed to answer my questions about name, address, and the like. His wife, however, had absolutely no English at all, and did not even respond to the word "hello." The class also seemed, to my ever more frantic eye, to include every stage between these extremes, with a young au pair from Spain, a Portuguese woman on the cleaning staff at the university, a couple of middle-aged European housewives, four or five first-year university students from Hong Kong, a Yugoslavian beauty therapist, two young brothers from Uruguay, an elderly Czechoslovakian gentleman, and an Iraqi machine operator.

At the time I could not imagine a more difficult class. It was a class I was quite unprepared to cope with, and I still blush at the memory of some of my more spectacular failures. The middle-aged Italian couple dropped out after only two classes. My attempt to get two Portuguese students to help each other backfired when it turned out that one came from the Azores and the other from the mainland. In my attempts to make sure that the university students still earned their course credit, I dragged the community people through activities quite inappropriate for their interests.

In an effort to offset these problems, I spent hours searching out and developing activities, putting in days of preparation for a two-hour class. The problem was that I still didn't know what I was looking for. Finally, in desperation and in what I considered at the time shameful defeat, I turned to the class and said, "This just isn't working. What are we going to do?" It was the first sensible thing I had done.

One of the themes of this book is that it is particularly important in a multilevel class that the students participate not only in the learning process but also in the planning and evaluation processes. For this to happen, the teacher of the multilevel class has to be prepared to let go of the notion that the teacher is the provider of all good things.

Teachers also have to recognize that there are many situations in which it is impossible to teach a perfect, or even a near-perfect, class. Many teachers feel guilt at what they perceive as their failure when students do not learn, and yet they may have been asked to cope with situations where the problems of a multilevel class are combined with those of large numbers, poor conditions, lack of equipment, inadequate preparation time, or imposed, unsuitable evaluation procedures. Looking back on the course described above, I sometimes wonder whether my biggest mistake wasn't in agreeing to teach the class at all. Although I certainly didn't realize it at the time, I was in fact lucky in one respect. This was in the years before the waves of refugees came to North America and before

Introduction

most of us in ESL faced the problems of adults with no literacy skills. All the students in my class were at least familiar with the letters of the roman alphabet, something that teachers today are unlikely to be able to count on.

My experience with a multilevel class is by no means exceptional. Teachers, many of them with little more experience than I brought to my class, are coping with equally heterogeneous classes every day. This book is intended to provide a practical guide for teachers facing mixed-level classes. I hope that it will be useful as a resource for practicing teachers and also as background in the field for teachers in training. It discusses the challenges and the advantages of the multilevel class and the problems inherent in developing a curriculum for a class with divergent abilities and interests. The book has a number of chapters on methodology, with detailed suggestions for activities and exercises that can be used with such classes. It shows teachers ways to adapt activities to suit the interests and abilities of particular classes, and gives suggestions on evaluation and assessment.

1

The Multilevel Class

When we talk about multilevel English classes, we tend to focus on the variation in the students' control of the language. We talk about the fluent student sitting next to the one who can barely piece together a sentence, or we compare the student who is learning the alphabet with the one who was a journalist in her own country. There is no doubt that varying language abilities in English are one of the dramatic challenges facing the teacher of the multilevel class, but they are not the only, or even necessarily the most important, way in which students may differ from one another.

A typical multilevel class

Let's look at a typical multilevel ESL class. It is an evening class held twice a week in a classroom of a public school in a large city. It is the only ESL class held in the evenings in this area, and it attracts anyone who has commitments in the daytime. The most vocal member of the class is Hector, a man in his early thirties from Uruguay. He works as shop-floor manager in a company that makes kitchen cabinets. His education is excellent, and he enjoys challenging the teacher about fine points of grammar. He really doesn't need to come to evening classes, but he has no family in this country and enjoys the social side of the classes. Another well-educated student is Nguyen, a Vietnamese doctor who is working as a medical orderly in the daytime. Nguyen's fluent French often proves helpful to him, especially in written work, but despite his educational background he is quiet and does not volunteer much. The teacher is not yet sure whether his silence is due to trauma or natural reserve.

The class also includes Johnny, a young man from Hong Kong, plus his father, a man who looks much older but may well be only in his fifties. On the days when his father doesn't come, Johnny is one of the stars of the class. When his father is there, however, he is more reticent. Another Chinese student is Mrs. Lim, an elderly lady who has been coming to class for three years now with very little noticeable improvement in her spoken English, although she tries very hard and even asks for written homework on a regular basis.

Rosa, a Spanish woman in her late forties, works as a waitress in the daytime. Her spoken English is fractured, but rapid and forceful, as her teenage children refuse to speak Spanish in the home. Her written English, however, is restricted to taking orders in the restaurant. Sisuvan is a young Laotian woman who is making exceptionally rapid progress in English. She is determined to learn; as well as coming to this class, she attends classes every morning in an adult upgrading program. The class also includes two Ecuadorean sisters, whose previous educational experience was restricted to a couple of years of grade school. They are not literate in any language and are making slow progress.

Others in the class include two Italian manual laborers who have lived in the city for nearly twenty years, a young Polish woman who worked as a clerk before leaving Poland but who is now fully occupied at home with two small children, a Jewish couple from Russia, and an Iraqi storekeeper.

There is no fee charged for the class, which is run on an open-entry open-exit system by which students may enroll anytime and drop out whenever they wish. Attendance tends to be irregular, with factors such as overtime, family or childcare problems, or simple fatigue after a day's work taking their toll.

Factors to consider

The students in this class vary in their level of English; however the teacher needs to take a number of other critical parameters into account in planning lessons as well. We can group these factors into those pertaining to the student's previous experience with education, those relating to the country and culture of origin, those relating to the individual student's personality, and those relating to the student's situation in North America.

Previous experience with education

At its simplest, variance in educational background means that some students have more experience in the classroom than others. They have acquired and developed learning strategies that they can bring to the task of learning a new language in a classroom setting; they are thus likely to make more rapid progress than those students who have had minimal or no exposure to formal education. This is not to imply that students with no exposure to formal classrooms have not developed any learning strategies, but there are learning skills related to formal education that are unlikely to be acquired elsewhere.

Literacy skills fall into this category. If the students' educational background includes literacy skills, even if in a completely different script, they have developed a whole set of skills, such as the ability to predict or to draw information from physical context, that will

transfer to the new language. Also, educational experience helps the students to feel at ease in the classroom. They are neither nervous nor disruptive, because the classroom routines fulfill their expectations. Such students are not baffled by teaching methods like the Socratic question-and-answer, in which the teacher obviously knows the answer but asks the question anyway. They are able to recognize that a task may have a learning-related goal that is not immediately obvious, and they have a more realistic expectation of the amount of time required to fulfill a learning objective.

If their experience extends to other languages or to a detailed study of their own language, they are likely to have the metalinguistic knowledge to hypothesize about the new language they are learning, to notice, for example, that "ed" is added to many verbs when describing completed actions and to hypothesize that this indicates past tense. All these skills make language learning easier for students who have a strong educational background. The teacher is likely to find that such students are ready and eager to move on to new material while other students are still struggling.

Country and culture of origin
The culture of the student's educational background also plays a role in student progress. Quite apart from the amount of previous education, the type of education is also significant. In some areas of the world the student role is seen as essentially a passive one. Students are raised to regard the teacher as the source of knowledge and the ultimate authority. To question the teacher in any way would be an insult to the teacher's authority. A student's role is to absorb whatever the teacher presents, not to critically evaluate it. Despite the fact that they are now adults, students raised under such a system may still come to the learning process with the expectation that the teacher will control the class absolutely and that their role will be restricted to one marked largely by rote memorization.

Mrs. Lim, the elderly Chinese lady, is a case in point. She works diligently at any exercises assigned by the teacher and joins in any choral work. She very rarely volunteers a question or comment, however, and is uneasy at being singled out for anything other than a straightforward response to a teacher query. She is happiest when the teacher works from a textbook; she can then predict what will come next and, if necessary, prepare for it. She gets upset when other students challenge the teacher or act in a way that she considers overly familiar.

The Russian students are particularly likely to upset her in this regard. Their educational system encourages students to volunteer knowledge, to challenge and to criticize. They consider that by constantly asking the teacher questions they are demonstrating their interest and grasp of the subject matter under discussion. They do expect strong class discipline, though, and are a little disconcerted when the teacher grins at latecomers rather than rebuking them, or makes no attempt to prevent the two Ecuadorean students from using their native language when they are stuck on a problem.

Such different expectations of what should happen in a classroom have to be borne in mind when the teacher is planning activities. Students will learn to adapt to different systems, but they may need different supports to help them do so.

A student's native culture can have other effects on classroom interaction, namely on the student's behavior roles. Hector, the Uruguayan, delights in teasing his young female teacher. He probably wouldn't try this tactic with a male teacher. Men from cultures where women are subordinate will not be used to having women as teachers and may take awhile to adapt to this. Also, some older students may find it hard to adapt to a much younger teacher.

The students' perception of their role is not restricted only to their interaction with the teacher. Women students may initially find it difficult or embarrassing to interact in mixed-sex groups, or they may hesitate to challenge male students even when the activity requires them to do so. Younger students may be similarly reluctant to disagree with older students and may feel it is impolite to speak up in the presence of their elders. This is why the performance in class of Johnny, the young Hong Kong student, is so variable. When his father is present, Johnny rarely volunteers a remark, deferring to his father even though the latter's command of English is much weaker than his own. In fact, Johnny finds language learning easy and in his father's absence, released of the cultural role demands, is happy to participate fully.

Students' interactions with each other can also be affected by political or status factors. In classes with students from a variety of nations and backgrounds, all too often the teacher finds that representatives of opposing groups are present. Perhaps it is students from a country where the north is considered superior to the south or the mainland to the islands. A student who comes from what is generally considered the inferior region often cannot resist prodding a supposedly superior student whose weaker language skills reverse the roles. More seriously, students may represent countries with severe political differences. In the class above, the teacher will need to watch out for problems between the Polish student and the Russians, and between the Vietnamese and the Laotian.

Another key factor related to the country of origin is the native language. As will be shown in the chapters on methodology, a spread of native languages can be one of the positive features of the multilevel class. Nonetheless, the teacher must be prepared to deal with the fact that students with languages that share common ancestry with English will find learning easier than those whose native language is widely different. Chinese students, for example, have no equivalent for "the" or "a" in their language, and will find these difficult to learn. For most European students this task is one of the easiest parts of English. Similar problems exist with pronunciation, grammar, the writing system, and sociocultural behavior. These are all areas in which the demands are greater on the Asian students than on the Europeans; their progress will be affected accordingly, all other things being equal.

Individual factors
We should not forget the importance of individual factors such as age, intelligence, and motivation. Students are individuals, and the teacher should be very wary of racial stereotypes. Younger students generally find learning less difficult than older students do and are more flexible about adapting to new methods of learning. Some students are highly intelligent, others less so. Some may appear to be less intelligent than others when in fact they are not getting the opportunity to learn in their preferred learning style. Perhaps they need to see things written down, but they are enrolled in a class where the teacher prefers a more oral approach. Maybe they like a highly structured classroom and are ill at ease without a clear sense of direction.

Some students in a class may be strongly motivated to learn

English and are prepared to work hard at the task. Perhaps, like Nguyen, their ability to regain their old position and resultant self-respect depends on requalifying in English. Other students, such as the Italian construction workers, may have very little need for English, working as they do in a trade where all everyday interaction takes place in their native language. After many years of residence in North America, they have picked up plenty of English for everyday needs like banking or shopping. They don't have any clearly defined goals for their learning, just a general feeling that it's always good to improve one's English. If pressed, they will admit that they see the day coming when their children will marry English speakers, but the need is hardly urgent yet. Their goals are therefore not clearly defined. Rosa, in contrast, knows exactly what her goal is. She wants to take a training course in hairdressing, and knows that her written English is not good enough. She has no interest in spoken activities and wants to focus all her attention on reading and writing.

The student's attitude to the new country is also critical. The wife who had no wish to leave her own home but who had to accompany her husband may be more interested in maintaining her children's command of the native language than in learning English. Refugees who have reluctantly fled their own land but who hope constantly to return may not be ready to make the commitment to a new country implied by job retraining or even serious language learning. Alternatively, those who were glad to escape with their lives and feared statelessness may be strongly motivated to work for citizenship at the earliest possible moment and to reestablish themselves here.

Situational factors

Unlike children in a classroom, who have learning as their primary job in life, adult ESL students regard learning as just one more thing to fit into their daily routine. The amount of time and effort students can devote to the task will vary enormously, as will the amount of support available. Many ESL students go home from the class to a milieu where the only place they hear English is on television. Their limited English competence means they tend to work in jobs that demand little in the way of interaction in English. Many of them, such as the Italian construction workers, have chosen jobs in fields dominated by their language group, where their native language is the language of interaction. They may live in ethnic areas where interaction with neighbors, shopping, and other social and commercial interactions can all take place in the native language. Such students are unlikely to make progress as rapidly as those who work, live, or socialize in an English-speaking milieu.

The amount of time individual students can give to the task of learning is another variable. Most students try to juggle the demands of a job, a family, and their ESL classes. Any problem, such as a sick child or a busy period at work resulting in overtime, will make it impossible for them to attend class. Shift work is another common cause of irregular attendance, which will delay student progress and make it difficult for a student to follow any material presented on a sequential basis.

Another personal variable is length of time in the country. Recent arrivals have an urgent need for orientation information, such as how the local transportation system works or what the local school expects of them as a parent. Long-term residents have presumably sorted out such matters to their satisfaction, although changes in lifestyle can produce a sudden demand. A student may be faced with new challenges following the death of a spouse or the marriage of a child who previously handled certain tasks.

Reasons for multilevel classes

Multilevel classes are offered for a variety of reasons. In areas with few ESL students, mixed-level classes may be the only option. Sometimes students prefer a multilevel class, however, and will choose to attend one even in areas that offer classes at various levels.

Administrative benefits

Although a few large educational institutions have deliberately opted for heterogeneous grouping within their classes, for the most part multilevel classes are found in locations where only one or two classes must satisfy all comers. It is easy to see the administrative benefits. Few school boards and other institutions can afford to provide teachers at all levels of instruction when there may be only three or four students enrolling in each category. Setting up a multilevel class relieves them of the obligation to perform placement testing or to provide extra classes.

The Multilevel Class

Convenience for the learner

Many students, too, find small local multilevel classes attractive. Even in large cities, where ESL centers offer classes at all levels, there will be students who prefer to attend a mixed-level class in their immediate neighborhood. Classes may be selected because they are within walking distance or because they are held at a convenient time. The provision of daycare may be a critical consideration, as may the absence of a registration fee.

Some learners feel comfortable only in a bilingual class where they can be confident that the teacher will speak their own language. In areas with a wide ethnic mix, such classes rarely attract sufficient numbers to allow for more than one class in each language.

Companionship and support

These reasons, however, tend to explain why students tolerate mixed-level classes rather than why they seek them out. Many students do in fact prefer mixed-level classes, generally because they have friends or relatives who are also interested in learning English, and they want to be assured of being in the same class. Many teachers of supposedly homogeneous groups have met the situation in which a student insists on joining a class of inappropriate level because that is the one in which he or she has friends. Some students are shy and enjoy the moral support of a friend. Others may never have experienced monolingual instruction and want a more fluent speaker along to interpret if necessary.

Cultural roles may also encourage students to select multilevel classes. Johnny, the young man from Hong Kong, does not wish to be put in a class more advanced than the one in which his father is studying. Women from some cultures may be allowed to attend only if they are in a class with their husband or another relative as chaperone.

Problems of multilevel classes

As we have seen above, so many factors affect the learning rate of ESL adults that even classes grouped by ability tend to demonstrate a wide spread as time goes on. Irregular attendance is common in community classes, where average attendance is generally around two-thirds of registration. In other words, the teacher has to assume that one-third of the students missed whatever work was done in the previous class. The problems are aggravated in continuous-entry situations, when students can register and appear at any time. Such students not only miss the particular items taught in previous weeks, but also miss learning the structure, the routines and patterns of activities, and the expectations of the class.

All these factors will slow down the progress of the student and widen the gap between the original students and those who arrive later. Teachers who begin with an ability-grouped class are never going to face the great range of abilities of the one-room schoolhouse, but over time their students will develop a wide enough spread to make it difficult for the teacher to work simply from a preset syllabus. Some of the problems and solutions presented are thus applicable to all ESL learners, regardless of the label given to their classes.

Methodology

Teachers generally identify their biggest problem with multilevel classes as being one of techniques. "What can I give them to do that won't bore the advanced students and won't be too difficult for the beginners?" is a fairly common question. It's answered at some length in chapters 3, 4, and 5 on methodology.

Curriculum

In a class with fairly homogeneous levels of English ability, the first step in developing a curriculum would be the performance of a needs analysis, in which we discover what our students want to use English for. We identify their weak areas and assess what skills they already have. From the information we gather, we can decide which items should be covered in class and can develop an order of approach so that new items can build on those previously covered. Working with our students, we develop both short- and long-term objectives so that we can measure progress and assess the effectiveness of our program.

This is not so simple with a multilevel class. Let's look back for a moment at some of the students described earlier. Rosa, the Spanish waitress, wants to develop her reading and writing. Her initial reaction to questioning about her English needs would probably be to say that she felt no need for help in speaking English. She functions in English every day. If pressed, she would admit that she sometimes feels uneasy about her English in more formal settings, for instance when talking to her children's teachers. Far more important to her, though, is to be able to produce a piece of English writing of which she can be proud. She doesn't yet recognize that she needs accuracy exercises to improve the structure of her sentences more than she needs handwriting practice.

The two Ecuadorean sisters also want reading and writing, but at a very different level from Rosa. They barely know the letters of the alphabet. Nor do they have enough oral skills to give them much to write about in English. What they might really benefit from is a bilingual teacher to give them some literacy training in their native language and basic oral work in English. In addition, they need some orientation information. As relatively new arrivals, they need to find out about schools, hospitals, the job market, retraining possibilities, social services, transportation, and a lot of other things. Such information would also be useful to Sisuvan and a few of the other more recent arrivals, but would be of very little interest to the Italians or Mrs. Lim. The latter could really use some development of her listening skills and a lot of pronunciation practice.

How can a teacher possibly gather all these disparate threads together into a curriculum? This is the most serious problem of the multilevel class, and is considered more deeply in Chapter 2.

Group conflict

Another challenge for the teacher is to avoid the students' perceiving the mixed-ability levels as a problem. Students are very quick to measure the abilities of their classmates and to rank them. Lower-level students may feel intimidated by the competition and may not make the same effort that they would in a more homogeneous classroom. The more advanced students may feel that they are being held back and may become impatient with the beginners. Such problems can be exaggerated if there is a situation in which the different ability groups also reflect different cultural groups, particularly those traditionally opposed to each other. Mainland Portuguese, for instance, tend to be better educated than persons from the Azores. A class with a number of Portuguese students will sometimes contain a beginner group of Azoreans sparring with a more fluent group of mainlanders. To avoid such problems, it is critical that the teacher work hard to develop a group feeling in the entire class.

Assessment and evaluation

Assessment and evaluation tend to be neglected in a multilevel class. Many institutions offering a single multilevel class feel that placement evaluation is irrelevant, as there is only one class in which students can be placed. This attitude fails to take into account that such evaluation information is highly useful in developing curriculum and is critical in measuring the students' progress. Final evaluation at the end of course is also unusual in the multilevel class; few courses of this type are taken for credit or have any formal, preset examination at the end. In multilevel courses evaluation is primarily of value to the teacher in assessing the effectiveness of the program. In some programs, however, a decision may need to be made about the appropriate point to promote a student from the beginners class to the advanced class—a decision all too often made not on the basis of progress but on that of endurance.

Why is assessment so badly neglected in multilevel classes? Largely it is because of the difficulty of devising an evaluative instrument suitable for students with such varied backgrounds, skills, and goals. Certainly little of the standardized testing material commercially available is suitable, and few teachers have experience in developing their own assessment tools. Suggestions for ways to get program feedback and to measure student progress are given in Chapter 3.

Preparation

There is no doubt that a multilevel class makes heavy preparation demands on the teacher. Teachers of these classes cannot just pick up an assigned text and work through it. No textbook can foresee the combination of abilities, interests, and backgrounds that make up any particular multilevel class, so teachers are virtually forced to develop materials for their own students. Teachers working with such a class for the first time are likely to find themselves putting in disproportionate amounts of preparation time, although they will certainly find that the effort put into materials development will pay off for future classes. They will still be wise to explore all possible avenues of support, such as enrolling teacher's aides or asking for volunteers from the local high school. Teachers in some areas have negotiated successfully for extra paid preparation time for such classes. Other teachers have got together in self-help groups, swapping not only ideas but also actual materials.

Teacher attitude

Many of us feel we should be able to teach any class we are given and come out smiling. Sometimes we feel that it is our responsibility to make the students learn. The truth is that it is the students' responsibility to learn, and that there are some classes that no one should be asked to teach, for example classes that demand so much preparation time that the paid hourly rate comes down below the minimum wage. Both teacher and student are working in a context that has limiting factors that neither can control. The number of class hours, the size of the class, the students' home responsibilities, and their opportunities for English use outside of the class will all affect the learning process. We have to recognize that Superteach died of overwork and relieve ourselves of some of the burden of guilt when our students don't seem to be making the progress we would wish.

I'm not suggesting that we take the attitude, Well, I taught it so it's their responsibility to learn it. Rather, there are some things we cannot do for our students. We can find out what they need and are interested in. We can develop materials to match those needs and present them as interestingly and clearly as possible. But we cannot

learn for our students. In fact, by trying to take on the entire responsibility, we are short-changing our students and failing to acknowledge their crucial role in the learning process. As adults they will determine their own learning patterns. They have to set their own goals and decide for themselves how much time and effort they want to devote to the learning process. It is up to them to make an effort to try new activities and methods, and to provide their own discipline in such areas as falling back on the native language or attempting assignments. These are not children who need guidance. They are adults whose learning will reflect the degree to which they are involved in the process.

Let the students set their own learning objectives. Let them decide what topic they want to work on and for how long. Tell them exactly what you are planning to do in a lesson and why. Let them tell you at the end whether they felt it was successful and why. If not, why not? Explain to them the limitations of the mixed class and ask them for suggestions as to how the problems might be overcome.[1] Chapter 3 on evaluation and assessment will discuss this in more detail.

Not all students will find it easy to make the transition to taking active responsibility for their own learning, particularly those who come from cultures where education is essentially a passive process. Faced with such students, the teacher will need to withdraw support gradually and stress the language-learning benefits of new methods. Students will feel more confident about attempting changes if the classroom is seen as a low-risk environment. In other words, a friendly, reassuring atmosphere becomes especially important when the students are first learning to take responsibility themselves. Another factor that can make changes less threatening is group approval. People who have learned to trust each other are more prepared to try out new behavior patterns than individuals are, so the development of bonds between the students will help the teacher.

The teacher also has to bear in mind that it is impossible to be all things to all people. There will always be students who want more of your individual time than you can give. We cannot overcome all the limitations of a wide variety of abilities in one class, and we shouldn't get upset when we run into one of those limitations. At times some students will sit idle while you spend longer than you planned getting another group organized. That's the way it goes. It doesn't mean the teacher is a failure.

Advantages of multilevel classes

Sometimes it's hard to believe that there are any advantages to a multilevel class, but in fact there are some and it is our job to make

---

1. The teacher obviously wants to be careful that encouraging feedback does not lead into a destructive criticism session. As one of the reviewers of this manuscript pointed out, "Some students may become increasingly negative and project their frustrations with language learning onto the class; some may begin interrupting the ongoing process to question that process to such an extent that the interruption will jeopardize the process; some may become personal in criticizing the teacher, the program, and the other learners, inappropriately comparing them with others. The teacher needs to be prepared for these possibilities and be prepared to set ground rules for getting this feedback." These cautionary remarks are valid, but should not deter the teacher from encouraging student involvement. Setting up special evaluation times, such as at the completion of a lesson or activity, and making it clear from the outset that personal remarks about other students are not acceptable will keep problems to a minimum.

the most of them.

Flexibility
One of the most common advantages is that the teacher is unlikely to be forced into teaching a set syllabus. This may not seem to be much of a consolation, but if you talk with high school foreign-language teachers, whose every lesson is committed to a race to complete the set text before handing the class over to the next year's teacher, you begin to realize that being able to go wherever your students' interests take you is a very attractive proposition. Someone can lend you a computer for a couple of weeks? Great! Your students would love to try it out—the high school French teacher doesn't have time. Fancy a class trip to the local theater or a day out at a nearby attraction? Your syllabus is flexible. You can turn all these activities into useful, interesting lessons. Not so the teacher with a specified syllabus.

Marching hand in hand with rigid syllabi are external examinations. Very few multilevel teachers have to worry about covering a certain amount of material in order to give their students a fair chance at an examination. Teachers working with preuniversity students attempting the TOEFL test may not face the range of abilities you do, but they are completely locked into the pressure of covering what will be tested, and woe betide the teacher who tries to stray from the prescribed subject matter. Our students are prepared to trust us to provide useful, relevant material without all the emotional pressure of examinations.

Diversity
Multilevel classes can be unusually relaxed, friendly places. In part because of the lack of external pressures but also because of the very mix of people involved, those who would normally be uneasy in a classroom can bring along moral support in the form of a friend, relative, or interpreter. The very variety of age, race, and background leads to interesting differences in viewpoint and experience, so that natural interactions are possible between students. The different language abilities mean that there are always some students with sufficient fluency to initiate conversations or begin social interactions. The mix of cultures guarantees that the entire class won't sit passively silent.

A number of activities can be attempted only in multilevel classes. In some cases the demands made on the participants are uneven, as in games like Twenty Questions, in which one person has to formulate all the questions and the other merely has to say yes or no, or in roleplay situations where one role is dominant. Such activities work extremely well in multilevel classes. In other activities the task may call for group leaders, as for instance with small-group listening activities. The skills of the advanced students can be put to good use here, while the lower-level students are still challenged too.

Interaction

There are also advantages for the individual student. Beginners have the opportunity to call on a wide range of potential helpers rather than relying solely on the teacher. In many cases, they can even ask for this help in their native language if they are having difficulty. The advanced students get the satisfaction of demonstrating their prowess and the opportunity to check their control of language items by attempting to teach them themselves.

Having students from a variety of language backgrounds is an unqualified plus, as they must fall back on English as a medium of communication. Such tasks as deciding who will be responsible for coffee cleanup become valuable language-learning activities, and of course the coffee break itself becomes an integral part of the lesson. Students will also give each other important feedback about pronunciation and intelligibility, without the misleading effects of sharing the same accent.

The final advantage is that a multilevel class can encourage students to grow in much more than just English. A wide range of talents and interests is likely to be displayed in the class, and students can bring stories, insights, and skills from all sorts of different backgrounds. All these differences contribute to a lively, fascinating classroom.

2

Planning a Curriculum

The problem of which teachers tend to be most aware when faced by a multilevel class is that of providing challenging, useful activities for all class members simultaneously. Unfortunately this approach can lead to the selection of a variety of activities that may be valuable in themselves but that may not in the long run add up to the most productive use of the students' time. We really have to look at our program over the long term and ask ourselves these questions: What can these students achieve in the time available? What do they need most? Which of those needs can I cover, given the limitations of the class? What objectives are reasonable to set and hope to have fulfilled? What progress will have to be shown in order for the students and me to judge this class to have been a success?

The answers to these questions involve us in designing our own syllabus and curriculum,[1] as it is immediately obvious that we cannot rely on any commercially available text to select our teaching items or decide our order of approach for us. This is not as difficult as it may sound, as we will see if we begin practically by looking at one way in which a multilevel class can be organized.

A sample class

Let's look more closely at the multilevel class described in Chapter 1, in which the students vary in age, cultural background, literacy

---

1. I am using the term *syllabus* to refer to the selection of items that will be taught and the term *curriculum* to refer to the fleshing out of a syllabus to include approaches, activities, and methodology.

skills, oral abilities, previous education, and personality. Yvonne, the teacher of this class, is an experienced instructor and has organized her program around a number of themes, or subject areas of interest to her students. This particular lesson is part of a food theme that Yvonne had begun the week previously.

Yvonne arrives early and does her best to set the public school classroom up to look inviting for her students, despite the fact that it is designed for ten-year-olds and many of the desks are unsuitably small. As she drags the desks into clusters of six, she reminds herself to nag the night school principal one more time about getting her permission to use one of the other rooms where the chairs and tables are more suitable for the adults in her class.

She greets all the students as they arrive, making a point of chatting to the basic students, getting them used to social patterns of interaction even though they do not understand her language. Once most of the class has arrived, she shifts from individual conversations to addressing the whole group, pulling everyone into her comments on Rosa's new hairstyle and Johnny's new shirt, and asking whether xanyone knows anything about two students who have not shown up.

When the social chat is exhausted, she pulls out a large colored picture of a family in a pizza restaurant, which she got by writing to the head office of the chain and asking for any outdated advertising material. She asks the class to describe what they can see, initially addressing the newest students and writing on the board the single words or simple factual phrases, such as "family" or "they eating," that are offered. Higher-level students comment on the waitress serving the food, the people in the background of the picture, and the fact that the little boy has got pizza sauce on his nose. Yvonne makes no attempt to record these lengthy sentences but does add some of the key vocabulary items to the board.

Some of the beginners listen to these exchanges: others, such as the two sisters from Ecuador, are busy copying the words from the blackboard. As Yvonne turns her attention to the most fluent students, she guides them to comment on the social patterns suggested by the picture. Topics such as children's behavior in a restaurant, ways of attracting a waiter's attention, and tipping are touched on. One of the Italian men comments that North American families eat out a lot, which provokes surprise from some of the Oriental students, who feel they ate out more frequently at home. This leads into a general discussion about fast food and the types of items that are available in the different countries. Everyone joins in this, if necessary resorting to translation, listing ingredients, and even making quick chalk drawings on the blackboard to get their points across.

When all the students have had a chance to contribute to this discussion, Yvonne moves on to the next phase of the lesson. She asks the three beginners with minimal literacy skills (Marta and Carmela from Ecuador and Yusefi from Iraq), to pair off with the three most advanced students (Hector, the shop-floor manager from Uruguay; the young Hong Kong student, Johnny; and Larissa, the Russian woman). She tells the literacy-level students to dictate descriptions of the restaurant picture that will be transcribed without correction by the advanced students, who will then help the beginners read it back. Yvonne makes it clear to the advanced students that they will be asked to correct the material later, thus trying to avoid their turning the transcription task into a grammar lesson, although she knows from experience that they will not be able to resist helping the descriptions along a little. She makes sure that Hector works with Yusefi, as she suspects that the sisters will fall back on using Spanish too much if she allows them to work with a Spanish speaker, although she is grateful for Hector's ability to translate her instructions and thus get the activity off to a good start. Yusefi's listening skills are still quite limited, and he looks a little baffled initially but soon catches on once he sees Marta and Carmela at work.

Yvonne then sets to work with the middle group, creating a language experience story based on the oral work done with the picture. She asks each student to contribute a sentence describing some part of the picture; she records the sentence on the board, reading it back as she does so. She works with the text that the group has created, asking students to read out certain words or sentences depending on their level. Then she rubs out some words and phrases and gives the chalk to the students to write them in again.

The text contains a number of errors, some of which go unnoticed, some of which get pointed out by more fluent students. A typical sentence is "Woman asking waitress more coffee." Yvonne decides to work with this sentence in more depth and do some structural work.

She writes the sentence on a clean piece of blackboard and

gives the students a chance to correct it before she demonstrates the correct form herself. She works with this pattern for about five minutes, using a pattern table to show how different words can be substituted into the content slots to produce such other sentences as "The child is asking her mother for more candy" and "The government is asking the people for more money." Finally she asks the students to copy the experience story from the board while she organizes the next activity.

She tells the three advanced students to make their own copies of the beginners' stories, take them away, correct them, and develop extra paragraphs comparing the North American scene portrayed in the restaurant picture with a typical restaurant scene from their own country. Once they have completed the first draft of this written assignment, they are to read the stories to each other for critical feedback.

The three beginners watch Yvonne as she hurries to lay out the next activity for the middle group, a pair exercise involving giving and following oral instructions. One partner of each pair is given a sheet on which are glued twelve pictures of food items cut from advertising fliers. The other student has the same pictures jumbled in a pile, and must follow the partner's oral instructions to achieve the same arrangement as on the sheet. Once the task is completed, both partners compare results to see how accurate they were, and swap their game with that of another pair of students.

While this is going on, Yvonne returns to the beginners and looks at the language experience stories that they have dictated. She suspects that the first few sentences are those most likely to have been genuinely produced by the beginners and accordingly focuses her attention there. She selects for pattern practice a sentence that occurs in similar form in all three narratives, "Family in restaurant," and expands it to "The family is in the restaurant."

Working with this small group of beginners, her goal is to develop word-recognition skills as well as to teach the structural pattern. Instead of using the blackboard, as she did with the middle group, she writes each word of the sentence on an individual card. These can be turned face down to focus attention on a particular word, or the cards for the whole sentence can be shuffled and reordered by the students. When the students demonstrate that they can recognize the individual words and recreate the basic sentence

22

pattern, Yvonne writes out a few extra word cards to substitute for the words "family" and "restaurant." The students are thus introduced to all the variations of "The mother/father/child is in the restaurant/store/house."

After this the class takes a coffee break. The advanced students come up to Yvonne and show her what they have been working on. She tells them she will take their work home and look at it more closely, but gives an initial encouraging comment before suggesting they all go for coffee together. She is aware that the advanced students haven't had much individual attention today so makes a point of drinking her coffee with them and encouraging them to talk.

After the break, Yvonne sets out some self-access material[2] that she has prepared related to the theme of food. She has gathered exercises and activities from a variety of sources, and she will let the students choose what they want to work on. Gathering this material is time-consuming, but because of the amount of choice involved, she can put out the same materials on three or four occasions. She also swaps materials with other teachers, thus reducing the preparation load. On this occasion she puts out activities that focus on listening, speech, reading, writing, and accuracy.

For listening, she has recorded a conversation in a butcher's shop in which the price of a number of items is asked. Two different tasks accompany the tape. One is a partially completed table of items and prices that requires the listener only to identify a few prices. The other is a set of comprehension questions that ask not only for factual information but also for assessment of the customer's reactions to the prices and the butcher's reaction to the string of questions.

Speech activities to be done with a partner include suggestion cards for roleplays; dialogues cut into strips and scrambled to be re-ordered then read aloud; and information-gap activities, in which partners have to get information from each other.[3]

Reading and writing activities include comprehension exercises based on finding information from food advertisements or menus, and cartoons and short stories relating to the food theme.

Activities that focus on accuracy ask the students to match food pictures with vocabulary cards, to manipulate grammar patterns, or

2. See Chapter 8 for a detailed discussion of self-access material.
3. See Chapter 7 for a full description of information-gap activities.

to select socioculturally appropriate remarks to restaurant and sales staff.

Yvonne's students are used to this style of working and know what she expects of them. As they return from coffee, they wander around the room looking at what is available and select an activity that they think will be challenging and interesting. They are aided in their choice by the color-coded stickers that Yvonne has attached to the materials. These use the colors of the rainbow as a mnemonic, with red indicating the easiest materials. While the students choose their activities, Yvonne circulates, clarifying instructions or helping with the selection if necessary. Answers are provided on the reverse of the materials where necessary, so students can correct their own work and Yvonne can focus on explaining rather than marking. Some of the students select materials that are apparently unsuitable, and that may not seem to provide much challenge. By contrast, the Russian man takes the most difficult accuracy activity and spends a long period of time puzzling over the instructions. Yvonne leaves him alone and honors his choice as she does that of the other students.

The self-access materials keep the students occupied until the last few minutes of class, when Yvonne pulls everyone together again for a group discussion before the class finishes. She asks the students which activities they enjoyed most and which were most useful. The students don't necessarily agree. Many of the students in the large middle group say they enjoyed the game of matching food pictures, but the older Chinese man feels the pattern practice was the most useful and comments that the game of matching pictures was a waste of time. His son speaks to him in Cantonese, explaining the language goals of the game, but the older man remains unconvinced. Most of the students agree that they like the free choice element of the self-access material and ask if they can continue with the activity in the next class. Yvonne agrees to this and makes a note to incorporate it into her lesson planning before saying good-bye to the students.

Planning of the sample class

The most cursory glance over this description of a lesson will show us that Yvonne was able to provide activities that kept all the students occupied throughout the class. If we look more closely, however, we will see that the selection of activities was not random, but carefully orchestrated.

First, Yvonne wanted to provide enough variety to maintain interest, while limiting the content sufficiently to avoid information overload. She did this by providing a variety of different exercises but selecting a common theme of food throughout. The vocabulary items and certain structural patterns could thus be recycled throughout the varied activities. This made the language demands easier for the beginning students without restricting the more advanced students. As we can see from the following chart, despite the variety of activity the language focus is quite tight.

Activity	Language focus
Social chat	Use of social formulae Advanced: Sociocultural interaction
Describing picture	Food and restaurant vocabulary Advanced: discussing sociocultural norms
Dictating story about picture	Food and restaurant vocabulary Structures using present and present-continuous tenses
Pattern practice	Structures using present and present-continuous tenses
Matching picture game	Food vocabulary Present-tense structures, including imperatives
Writing about food	Advanced: Sociocultural norms in own culture
Self-access material	Food vocabulary plus student-selected focus

Another feature, shown in the chart below, is the arrangement of groupings to capitalize on the benefits of the multilevel class.

whole-group activities	social chat
	describing picture
	final wrap-up
equal-ability groups	pattern practice
	matching picture game
	writing and editing each other's work
cross-ability groups	transcribing stories
	some self-access activities
individual work	self-access activities

To build up group unity, Yvonne made sure she incorporated certain activities in which the whole class worked as a unit despite the variety of abilities and backgrounds. Activities such as talking about a visual stimulus allow students to contribute at their own level and thus are suitable for the whole group. She recognizes, however, that certain tasks, such as teaching grammar, are firmly linked to a particular ability level. To provide that kind of input, therefore, she took advantage of the times when the class was grouped by ability. She also made use of the uneven nature of some tasks, such as transcribing someone else's story, to provide an opportunity for students of very different abilities to work together. This is valuable not only as a way of building group unity and providing some individual attention for the beginners but also because the "teacher" role tends to push the advanced students into a greater awareness of how the language operates and helps them to identify areas of their own expertise that need attention.

The exercises were also organized with regard to the type of activity. Yvonne's long-term planning incorporates the four basic skills (listening, speaking, reading, and writing) plus pronunciation work, sociocultural awareness, and orientation information for those who need them. She knows that not all these will necessarily be covered in every lesson, but she nonetheless tries to provide a balance of the skills with extra emphasis on students' weakest skill areas. In this lesson, the breakdown of activities by skill is shown in the chart below.

Activity	Level		
	beginner	intermediate	advanced
social chat	listening sociocultural	speaking and listening sociocultural	speaking and listening
describing picture	oral/vocab orientation	oral	oral/ sociocultural
language experience story	speaking reading	speaking reading	transcription writing (including editing)
pattern practice	writing	writing	
matching picture game	listening	speaking	
writing about own culture and editing other's work		writing speaking listening reading	

As the table demonstrates, the lesson provided practice in the basic skills for students at all levels. It did not, however, cover pronunciation; Yvonne will note this in her evaluation of the lesson and make sure that this area receives attention in future lessons.

Related to this question of providing a balance of activities in the various skill areas is the purpose of those activities. The term "speaking activity," for example, can be used to cover everything from discussing another student's piece of writing to a choral repetition drill. The first activity is done without any supervision from the teacher, and the measure of its success is whether or not the writer can be persuaded to amend his or her copy without offense being given. In other words, the focus of the activity is on using the language not for its own sake but for the purpose of achieving something; that is, on the meaning of what is said, not on the form of words chosen.

The drill, by contrast, focuses firmly on the form of the words. It is done under supervision, and its success is measured by how closely the form is reproduced, not by the meaning of what is said. Generally speaking, we do activities of this type to improve students' accuracy, to teach them new language forms, and to correct errors. Accuracy exercises need not focus only on grammatical points. An activity that requires students to recognize the degree of formality in a conversation or that asks them to produce polite and impolite refusals is also an accuracy activity, because the students' attention is focused on the form of the words being chosen, rather than on the meaning of the words.

Students need both accuracy and fluency activities, of course. An initial focus on form allows them to recognize the learning point and focus on it. Unfortunately, simply knowing a rule doesn't always mean it can be used in real life. Too often, when we are really trying to communicate and our focus is on the meaning of what we are saying or hearing, we forget all about these learned rules. We need a chance to try out this knowledge in as real a situation as possible where we can measure our success by how well we get our message across. Fluency exercises allow for this.

Yvonne's planning incorporated both kinds of activity, as this chart shows.

Activity	Language focus
Social chat	Fluency
Describing picture	Fluency (offering spontaneous comments) Accuracy (checking out sentence structures with teacher)
Dictating story about picture	Fluency

Pattern practice	Accuracy
Matching picture game	Fluency
Writing about food	Fluency (giving information) in own culture Accuracy (editing)
Self-access material	Accuracy or fluency at own choice

Yvonne's selection of activities was certainly not random but was the result of careful planning that incorporated a number of basic principles of syllabus and curriculum design.

Syllabus development

Let's look more closely at how this lesson was developed. Yvonne's first step concerned syllabus, that is, the selection of teaching items and the order of their presentation.

Hierarchical syllabus

Teachers with fairly homogeneous classes can, if they wish, avoid the problems of syllabus design by selecting a class text and allowing that to determine the syllabus.

Yvonne rejected that idea for her class. Most class texts are organized around some form of hierarchical syllabus, in which the material presented in any given lesson assumes that the student has worked with and understood previous units. The hierarchy may be determined by structural language patterns, with students being taught, for instance, affirmative statements before being asked to apply a given rule to create negative ones. Other hierarchies are based on vocabulary; each subsequent lesson presupposes the knowledge of any vocabulary items introduced earlier.

These approaches are almost impossible to implement in a multilevel classroom. Because hierarchical texts have a specific point of departure, the teacher is faced with the problem of choosing between an elementary or more advanced text. The elementary book will not presuppose knowledge the basic level students do not have but will contain little to challenge the more advanced students. With a more advanced book, the beginners will need intensive help to provide the missing knowledge. Commonly, teachers put in this position compromise, select a text that suits the middle of the class, and try to adapt the exercises to suit individual students.

Hierarchical texts also make it difficult to develop objectives for individual students, because the objectives for the lesson are so clearly delineated by the hierarchy that they are not easily adapted.

Functional syllabus

There are some nonhierarchical approaches to syllabus design, although published text books have tended to favor the hierarchical approach. In recent years we have seen a number of textbooks organized on functional lines, a principle that need not be presented hierarchically, although it sometimes is. The language is selected and presented according to the purpose or function for which it is being used. Thus "May I have a cup of coffee?" and "That coffee

smells delicious!" might be presented together as ways to make a request, irrespective of the fact that they use quite different grammatical forms to make the request. It is apparent that functions can be fulfilled with different degrees of complexity. We might ask for directions with a simple question like "Where is the post office?" or

"Excuse me, I'm looking for the post office. I wonder if you could tell me where it is, please?"

Although functionally based textbooks tend to be written with a fairly specific student audience in mind, and any one book is therefore unlikely to suit all the students in a multilevel class, the functional syllabus does offer more flexibility than the hierarchical approaches described above. In a class such as Yvonne's, students could work on the same function but at different degrees of complexity. For instance, she could plan a unit on the topic "refusing an invitation" and set the following objectives for students at different levels:

Beginners: Learn a set phrase such as "I'm sorry, I can't."

Intermediates: Produce a reason for the refusal as well as the apology.

Advanced: Recognize the degree of formality in the invitation, select an appropriate apology, phrase the excuse in the desired degree of formality, and offer an alternative suggestion.

Although this particular example adapts to a multilevel class very well, not all functions are so simple to work with. Some, such as persuading, can only be realized with fairly high-level language and are normally only approached after considerable work has been done with other functions. There is thus some hierarchy even

in a functional syllabus, so Yvonne finds that function alone cannot give her the organizing principle she needs.

In common with many teachers, Yvonne finds, in fact, that she is instinctively uneasy with a rigid, preset syllabus because it does not provide her with the flexibility she wants for exploring areas of particular interest to her students. Many students are reluctant to state their needs on first arrival in a classroom and will only open up after they have come to trust the teacher and the group. Other students may never have given conscious thought to the question of what they want to learn, and have arrived with some vague notion of learning more English. This lack of initial information can make it very hard for the teacher to determine a syllabus in advance if the syllabus is perceived as a set body of knowledge to be taught and learned. The problem is exaggerated with a multilevel class, where it sometimes appears that one needs a different list of items for each student.

Process syllabus[4]

An alternative to listing language items is identifying those process-es that are involved in the use of language. For example, among many other things we need to be able to express information con-cisely, to listen for the main idea, and to produce comprehensible pronunciation. Regardless of level, students can usefully work for improvement in these areas. A process syllabus is one that identifies the processes that students will practice rather than the language items they will produce. The objectives of such a syllabus are there-fore expressed in terms of the skills and abilities that the students will develop.

Let's look at some of the skills and abilities that we would want to include. At the simplest level we would want to decide on our balance of reading, writing, speaking, and listening. Do the students have an equal need for all four of these skills, or are some learners already strong in one area? Then we have to break these skills down further. What do we mean by speaking? Being able to express our-selves fluently? Accurately? Intelligibly? Maybe the speaking skills should be subdivided, and pronunciation added.

We don't always speak in the same way, either. We need to be able to judge when a formal tone is required, or when it would be out of place. We need to know how to be polite and how to recog-nize whether someone is being polite to us. We need to know to whom to be polite. In other words, we need some sociocultural knowledge to enable us to use the language appropriately. Nor is all speech chatty conversation. We need to be able to give clear di-rections, to talk on the telephone, maybe even to make public speeches. We might use speech to persuade, exhort, cajole, flatter, or insult. All of these should play a part in our syllabus.

We can break down the other skills in a similar fashion, but even then we have barely covered half of what we would want to give our ESL students. Some of them might require life skills, such as knowing how to get information and help. Problem-solving skills,

---

4. I am using the phrase *process syllabus* in a manner similar to that defined by N.S. Prabhu as a procedural syllabus (See K. Johnson, *Communicative Syllabus De-sign and Methodology*, Pergamon Press, 1982, for a description of Prabhu's work.). The term process syllabus, however, is also used to describe learning experiences in which the intention is not to study specific content but to engage in a learning process, through which learners discover for themselves. A good language process syllabus should allow for both types of learning.

such as hypothesizing, information gathering, and generalizing, may be needed. Recently arrived students will need to know how the system operates in North America, which agency to approach for help, what kind of service one can expect, or what is expected of citizens in their various roles as workers, parents, and neighbors. Learning skills may themselves be needed. Strategies like asking for clarification, which will help students learn outside of the classroom, will be critical for some students. Others will need to learn classroom routines, what the teacher expects of them in situations such as group work, or self-access study. Sociocultural and sociolinguistic skills will also be part of the syllabus, depending on the abilities our students bring with them.

The checklist for any class will vary according to the background and needs of the students. The following example was developed by Sandy Solomon and Sandy Katz of North York Board of Education for a mixed-level class that included secondary and adult students.

Listening

1. Listen and respond appropriately to oral instructions.
2. Listen and respond appropriately to each other in group and classroom discussions.
3. Listen to tapes and films and express opinions based on facts presented in films.
4. Watch for non-verbal communication, while listening to other speakers.
5. Listen to what is not being said.
6. Identify differences in tone, stress; watch for pauses, repetition, sentence fragments, and idiomatic, colloquial, and vulgar expressions.
7. Identify levels of formality, relationship of speakers, and conversational gambits.

Speaking

1. Select and use language appropriate to a given situation.
2. Give oral answers to general questions, using structures and vocabulary comprehensible to native speakers.
3. Express orally an opinion on material under study.
4. Contribute orally to classroom and group discussions.
5. Participate in situational roleplays.

6. Deliver an oral presentation based on research material.
7. Use nonverbal communication while speaking.
8. Use conversational gambits to narrate, persuade, interrupt, explain, etc.
9. Use different levels of formality, tone, and stress, according to relationship of speaker and listener.

Another interesting example is found in the Alberta Vocational Centre SB/LB Resource Manual.[5] This program is designed for beginning students with a minimum of formal education, but many of the objectives are equally valid with more advanced students. The section of the manual on objectives begins as follows:

> During the course, countless "working objectives" may emerge for each class or each individual student and individual standards may be set. As learning a second language is seen to be a long term struggle, mastery is demanded on only a few objectives, which can legitimately be expected to be attained by conscious learning if necessary. However, these are not terminal objectives, nor are they discrete building blocks. Most activities will have multiple implicit objectives, which may differ for each participant.

The SB/LB Resource Manual lists a wide range of objectives, only a few of which are reproduced below:

> Speak intelligibly
>   connect words
>   articulate final consonants
>   use appropriate stress, rhythm, and intonation
>   use fillers appropriately
>   speak slowly enough
>   speak loudly enough
> Understand rapid speech
> Accept errors and learn from them

---

5. P. Price and S. Montgomery, "SB/LB Resource Manual" (Alberta Vocational Centre, Edmonton, Alberta, 1985, Mimeographed). For more information contact ESL Department, Alberta Vocational Centre, 10215 108 Street, Edmonton, Alberta T5J 1L6, Canada.

Make accurate predictions
Infer meaning from context
Read/listen for main idea
Carry on a short conversation
Ask follow-up questions
Give expanded answers to questions
Borrow/return/lend items
Understand procedures (e.g., time table, cafeteria, etc.)
Share belief that "we're all in this together"
Ask necessary questions in order to complete task
Participate actively in class

Retroactive syllabus

Many ESL teachers prefer what is known as a retroactive syllabus. They group and classify their activities both before and after they have taught them. If the planned activities of the class are disrupted by the arrival of some new students, the distress of a student over some personal problem, or a freak storm that has everybody arriving drenched and distracted, the teacher has the freedom to go along with these events and exploit the learners' interest and concern. Time is available for the students to identify their own interests and concerns and to select their own activities.

At the end of the lesson the material and activities covered are reviewed to see which processes were practiced that day. This review should be done whether the teacher has departed from the intended activities or not. The teacher can then judge which skills have been adequately covered and which will require some conscious attention over the next few lessons.

Curriculum development

To develop the syllabus into a curriculum, the teacher must decide which activities will provide the best practice of the various skills and attitudes that the students need. It can be seen that the process-based syllabus leaves the teacher plenty of freedom for the information content of the activities, and that it can thus be linked to a theme- or content-based approach if the teacher wishes.

Theme-based curriculum

Yvonne used an approach based on the theme of food in the lesson described above. During the course of the year she and her students will work with a number of themes, which she finds a useful way of linking activities for all levels of students as well as an excellent introduction to sociocultural issues.

Yvonne feels it is important that the students play a part in selecting the themes they will work with. Accordingly, she always listens for topics that the students raise themselves. In such a mixed-level class this isn't always easy, but she also gathers information in other ways, such as having the more fluent students translate, noticing which topics are popular in the self-access material, or asking which television shows are watched.

Many adult ESL classes choose as themes orientation areas, such as health care, job searching, or the local transportation system. There is no necessity for themes to be tied to orientation, however, and teachers have developed interesting themes on topics such as soap operas, newspapers, holidays around the world, finding out about other students, and so on.

Themes in themselves do not provide any structure but do provide a way to flesh out a skeleton syllabus. In addition, the relation to the theme guarantees that certain language items will reoccur, thus providing a way for students to review previous material and have a chance to use what they have learned naturally. This is not to suggest that the teacher can randomly string together any activities so long as they relate in some way to the chosen theme. For example, a program that consisted solely of oral activities on health care would be neglecting the writing and reading skills. Exercises and activities related to completing new-patient information sheets or reading medicine labels would be an important addition to such a theme.

Certain themes will tend to provide skill practice in one particular area, for example a unit on the telephone would tend to focus heavily on listening and speaking skills. This can always be balanced by the choice of a subsequent topic that will put the focus elsewhere. What themes do offer the teacher is an opportunity to explore areas of interest for the students, a chance to set the language in an important real-life context, and a way of recycling previously covered language without the boredom of formal review. In a multilevel class themes also provide the teacher with a way of presenting initial material that is relevant to the whole class, but that can then provide spin-off activities at different levels for different students.

We have seen above how Yvonne planned such a unit on food. For a health-care theme, the teacher might start with a video clip from a popular hospital drama on television or a photostory in which a small child takes poison by accident.[6] Visual start-up activities like these will provide an opportunity for the whole class to work together initially and for the teacher to introduce some of the vocabulary of the theme. Such starters allow for follow-up activities that pursue the specific needs of the different groups. These could be as varied as sorting bottle labels into poisons and nonpoisons; listening to the video with the sound down and trying to recreate the mother's telephone call for the ambulance; rearranging the cut-up photos of the photostory and providing a one-line caption for each picture; completing a new patient hospital entry form on the child, based on the information given in the story; and searching through a first-aid book or medical encyclopedia for information on poisoning and methods of treatment. With such a range of activities from which the teacher can choose, it should be possible to develop a curriculum that provides all the students with the opportunity to attempt activities that are useful, relevant, and balanced.

Content-based curriculum
I like to draw a distinction between theme-based language teaching and content-based teaching or, as it is sometimes known in the school system, language across the curriculum. In a theme-based language class the focus is primarily on learning the language, and the content matter is used as a vehicle for the practice of English. In a content-based curriculum the students' attention is focused on the subject matter. For example, in schools, immigrant children who are learning math in English simultaneously develop their math skills and their English skills, even though no conscious attention is paid to the English studies. This is equally true of adults, and some very successful lessons are under way for multilevel classes with names such as ESL typing and ESL computer studies.

In recent years there has been a lot of discussion in ESL circles regarding the ways in which students develop fluency in a foreign

6. See J. Bell and K. Weinstein, *Health Care* (North York, Ontario: North York Board of Education, 1980).

language.[7] If we look back to the way in which we learned our native language, it is evident that no one attempted to lay out a formal curriculum for us. Our mothers didn't decide that we should learn the simple-present tense before the continuous-present tense, or that the function of refusing should come before the function of inviting. Instead, language was used to communicate information, and we processed it accordingly. Similarly, when we first began to

speak, our parents didn't correct the form of our utterances, but the content. If we said proudly, "Look, dog!", no one said, "No, no, that's wrong. You must say, 'Look at the dog,'" although they might well have modeled the correct form in their encouraging reply of "Yes,

7. See S.P. Corder, "The Significance of Learner's Errors," *International Review of Applied Linguistics* 5 (1967): 161–170; L. Selinker, "Interlanguage," *International Review of Applied Linguistics* 10 (1972): 209–231; and S. Krashen, "Formal and Informal Linguistic Environments in Language Learning and Language Acquisition," *TESOL Quarterly* 10 (1976): 157–168.

that's right, it's a dog; look at the dog." Correction would normally come only if the content were wrong: "No, that's not a dog; it's a cat. Look at the cat."[8]

Despite this lack of concentration on form and the lack of any conscious effort on our part to learn the language, we all grew up to have total control of the grammatical forms of our native language. This process of naturally picking up a language has been labeled acquisition, in contrast to the learned language that we may have gained through formal study. It is obvious that acquisition can also play a part in adult second-language learning, as is shown by the number of immigrants who never attend classes but nonetheless pick up a fair control of the language as the result of being exposed to it frequently. This knowledge has been gained when the attention is focused on the meaning of the communication rather than the form.

We have all had experience with students who have apparently learned an item well in class and can demonstrate that knowledge in tests and exercises, but who completely fail to use the knowledge when they are speaking naturally. This has led some researchers to suggest that formal study is of no help to spontaneous language production but is useful only in those situations where attention to correctness and lack of time pressure allows for the spontaneous utterance to be compared against the known rule. One proponent of this view, Stephen Krashen,[9] maintains that the following conditions are critical for the acquisition of language:

- The attention must be focused on meaning, not on form.
- The student must hear the language items in question frequently and in a form that can be understood. Krashen refers to this as comprehensible input.
- The student must have a low affective filter. By this, Krashen means that the student must be relaxed and at ease enough that he or she is not blocking out all the input. In tense situations, language acquisition is unlikely to take place.

At first glance, this might indicate that there is no need for the

8. Correction based on the form of the message may be given to older children of certain socioeconomic groups when they use forms such as "Me and Susie done it." What is being corrected in this case, however, is less the use of an ungrammatical form than the use of a low-status one.
9. Stephen D. Krashen, *Second Language Acquisition and Second Language Learning* (Oxford: Pergamon Press, 1981).

language teacher. All the students need to do is mingle with native speakers or listen to the TV and they will pick up the language naturally. This is not Krashen's contention at all. He points out that though the mother or other caretaker does not concentrate on the form of the child's utterance, she does select the language she uses to present a naturally simplified language pattern adapted to the child's level. She provides not merely input, but comprehensible input. This is the critical role of the second-language teacher: the provision of input within a range that can be understood by the learner, and the provision of opportunities for communication in which the focus is on the meaning of the communication rather than the form.[10]

Although many ESL authorities would quarrel with Krashen's assertion that teaching the form of the language produces no improvement in spontaneous language performance, most agree with him

10. See S. Krashen and T. Terrell, *The Natural Approach* (Hayward, Calif.: Alemany Press, 1983) for suggestions on encouraging acquisition in the classroom.

that activities that focus on meaning and communication play a critical role in the class, and that many activities that at first sight do not appear to have much language-learning potential are in fact wonderful opportunities for the students to use language naturally. For the teacher who is having great difficulty following a step-by-step syllabus because of the differing demands of the multilevel class, this is a very reassuring thought.

One problem of this approach is that the students themselves may consider language learning to be a matter of studying new items from textbooks and often do not recognize that they are in fact making progress by playing language games or doing other similar activities. A colleague tells of a student who was working on the computer playing an adventure game. He had spent a number of hours reading the fairly demanding text, entering responses, trying out strategies and asking her for suggestions and help. When at the end of this she asked him whether he felt the activity had been useful, he said that he didn't think so, except that he had learned a new item of vocabulary that he hadn't met before, the word "dungeon." It is difficult to clearly identify the other gains that one feels instinctively he must have made in those hours of operating exclusively in English, while concentrating so hard on the problem of escaping the dungeon. Because such gains are not easily quantifiable, students tend to ignore them; it is thus important that the teacher make it clear to the students that such activities are not a waste of time.

One final note of caution here. We must recognize that even if all the claims of the acquisition approach are valid, they do not relieve teachers of the demands of planning a program. Adult students are not small children who have no knowledge of the way a language works. Often they are busy hypothesizing about the underlying patterns of the language they are learning and want the rules explained to them. Even the strongest proponents of the acquisition approach acknowledge that a knowledge of the rules of grammar is useful for many students and enables them to monitor the accuracy of their utterances in situations, such as written work, where they have time to focus on form.

3
Assessment and Evaluation

One of the advantages of the multilevel class is that we are normally spared the kind of formal external final examination that so limits the curriculum. The absence of such an examination does not, however, mean that we do not need evaluation procedures, but rather that we have the freedom to develop procedures that are more suitable to the needs of our class. In attempting to select such procedures, we must clarify exactly what it is we are trying to evaluate. In a classroom program we will want feedback on the students, on our own performance, and on the effectiveness of the materials and approaches we have selected.

It is too late to discover when the course is finished that our approach was quite unsuitable, so we need to institute ongoing evaluation procedures so that we can adjust our approach to suit the class. Similarly, we don't want to wait until the course is over to discover that a particular student hasn't been making progress or has done well in one skill area but hasn't improved at all in another. We need this information as soon as possible so that we can adapt our teaching methods to try to rectify the problem. Likewise, it is too late to find out at the end of the year that a student should never have been in our class at all but should have been guided to a literacy class or a bilingual class. It is also too late then for us to realize that we can't measure progress because we aren't sure what skills a student had on arrival. Nor can we measure progress if we have not decided exactly what it is we have tried to achieve. The fact that we can point to some generalized improvement does not mean that the learners made the best progress possible in the time available.

For all these reasons it is important that we realize that evaluation and assessment must not come at the end of a program. Rather, evaluation begins even before the class does and continues on throughout the program. This is as important for teacher and program evaluation as it is for student evaluation.

The basic steps in a classic evaluation process are these:

- **Assess the needs.** Why did the students come to class? What do they hope to achieve? What do they know already?
- **Select goals and objectives.** Which of the needs seem most important? Which do the students feel are most important? Given the restraints of time, budget, resources, and abilities, which can be realizable in the given time?
- **Select measures of success.** How is it decided whether a goal has been achieved? Will the teacher assess it ? Will the student? How? Personal opinion? Examination? Successful performance of a task? Comparison of current production with earlier tape or writing?
- **Perform ongoing assessment.** Do the chosen goals still seem appropriate, or should they be modified? Is the time allotted to achieving the goals appropriate? Is progress being made toward the goals?
- **Modify program or approach if necessary.** Negative feedback is an indication that change is necessary. Pace, content, presentation, or even attitude may need to be changed.

Three major forms of student assessment are normally carried out in language classes: placement, ongoing assessment, and final summative evaluation.

Placement testing assumes that there is some choice as to the placement of the student. This is commonly not the case for students in a multilevel class. Indeed, the very existence of the multilevel class is proof that few choices exist. This does not mean that we should ignore assessment on arrival, but that we should be looking for different information. Our goal is to determine a student's point of entry so that we can later measure progress, not to match the student against some predetermined criteria so that we can choose between classes.

Final evaluation is likely to be largely irrelevant in most multilevel classrooms. Regular classes have final evaluation so that they can decide whether the students have reached a level of competence that would allow them to proceed to the next level of classes. These "exit criteria" are clearly determined by the entrance qualifications for the next level. Students in a multilevel class generally do not have a next level to proceed to. They stay with us as long as their interest or need lasts. Final evaluation is therefore merely the last stage in an ongoing assessment of performance, where a student's achievement is measured against his or her own previous performance rather than against any externally imposed criteria.

Let's look again at the model for evaluation discussed above. The process described naturally is easier with a class whose students all begin at the same point. How can one select goals for students of widely different abilities? What does one do if the feedback indicates that the pace is right for some students but inappropriate for others? How does one involve low-level students in their own ongoing evaluation? Let's look at the process from the point of view of a multilevel class.

Assessment of needs

Needs assessment essentially compares what the learner can already do with what the learner needs to know in order to operate satisfactorily. We must ask some questions before we can assess the needs of language learners.

- **Where do the learners need to use English?** Do they use English at work? What kind of situation do they work in? Do they interact with the public in their job or do they use English only with co-workers? Do they use English in stores and restaurants, at their children's school, or with in-laws? What kind of reading and writing do they do in English?

- **Do they need to be accurate when they use English, or is it more important that they make themselves understood?** Do the interactions they have described indicate that it is important to use correct English? Do they have to write much in English, which will indicate a need for accuracy? Do they use English with native speakers or as a lingua franca with other immigrants? What is their personal bias towards accuracy or fluency? Do they find grammatical mistakes embarrassing?

- **What kind of situations are most common?** Interactions that take place regularly, such as buying food, will take precedence over those that happen rarely, such as buying a house.

- **Which are most urgent or considered most important?** Some needs are only occasional but are perceived as critical because of their value to the learner. This category might include making emergency phone calls, handling sexual harassment on the job, or writing a letter of complaint about a long-standing grievance.

- **Do they need orientation information?** New immigrants will need information about facilities and services in the area, for example the bus system or banking hours. They also need more general skills about the ways in which the system runs in this country, such as how to get assistance, where to find information, and entitlement to benefits.

- **What sociocultural knowledge do they lack?** Making oneself understood is not just a matter of language but includes gesture, body language, recognizing the appropriate amount of formality and politeness, recognizing taboo subjects, and so on. It also includes knowledge of behavior patterns, such as expected speed of response to various applications or patterns in development of intimacy. For example, the learners may have lived in this country for many years but may still fail to recognize a signal that one party wants to end a conversation.

- **What role are they most likely to be in when using English?** Will they mostly be interacting with English-speaking commercial agencies such as stores, where the onus is on the seller to accommodate the limited linguistic command of the customer? Or do they need English for situations like job interviews, where success or failure will depend on their ability to express themselves?

- **What do the learners consider to be most important?** What do they want to learn? All the information gathered above has to be interpreted in the light of the learners' own perceptions of their needs. Adult students must be involved in their own learning and direct it as far as possible themselves. Learners who have never been asked to think about the learning process are inclined at first to leave the decision-making to the teacher. "I just want to learn English" or "Whatever you want to teach" are often their off-the-cuff reactions to queries about their objectives. If they are given the same opportunity for input a little later, they are frequently far more explicit about their needs and wishes; they had simply had no cause to formulate them beforehand. Being given a list of concrete tasks or skills on which they can focus also helps learners who have little previous goal-setting experience to clarify their preferences.

Gathering information from students of very limited language proficiency is extremely difficult. If the students are fully literate in their own language, it is possible to use a chart format in which the language demands can be kept to a minimum, as in this example.

SELF-ASSESSMENT CHART

How well do you use English now?
Mark the situations where English is most important to you.

Situation	Do you use English?	How much do you understand/say?				
		0%	25%	50%	75%	100%
1. With friends at work						
2. With bosses at work						
3. With neighbors						
4. In stores						

47

5. On buses						
6. At the bank						
7. At the doctor's						
8. At your child's school						
9. Reading the newspaper						
10. Watching TV						
11. Filling out forms						
12.						
13.						
14.						

Although the language demands are light here, the literacy demands are extremely high and assume a familiarity with the conventions of chart layout that would make this form impossible to use with those who are not literate in their native language. For such students the teacher can either turn the form into a series of verbal questions and record the answers herself, or fall back on the use of an interpreter. New students often bring someone along to interpret when they first arrive to register for a class, and this may prove to be the only chance the teacher has to get some useful background knowledge of the lowest-level students.

One can draw up a fairly lengthy initial registration form that can also function as a preliminary needs analysis and placement test. Depending on the student's ability, this could be presented as a written assignment, an oral interview with someone transcribing answers, or a native-language record of background. The problem with this information gathering is that to be faced on first arrival by what may appear to be an examination is extremely disconcerting and not likely to encourage student confidence. If the focus of the form is clearly the presentation of information about the students themselves, some of this anxiety may be reduced. A possible model for such a form would be the following:

Name _____

Address _____

Telephone number   work _____ home _____

Native country _____ Native language _____

Date of birth _____ Age _____

How long have you lived in this country? _____

Do you have a job? _____

What do you do? _____

Are you married? _____

Do you have any children? _____

Here are some places where people use English. Put a mark by the places where your English is OK.

at work
in stores
with neighbors
children's school
with friends and relatives
on buses and trains
at the doctor's office
at the hospital
on the telephone

Put a mark by the places where you want to use better English.

at work
in stores
with neighbors
children's school
with friends and relatives
on buses and trains
at the doctor's office
at the hospital
on the telephone

Where else do you speak English?_____

Can you read these in English?

bills
checks
newspapers
forms
business letters
manuals at work
notices
school reports

_____
_____
_____

Do you want to read these in English?

    bills

    checks

    newspapers

    forms

    business letters

    manuals at work

    notices

    school reports

    _____

    _____

    _____

Some teachers prefer to gather information in an oral interview with each student, and there is no doubt that this yields a much richer understanding of the learners' own feelings about the learning process. Unfortunately many teachers only meet their students en masse and have classes of a size that prohibits lengthy individual interviews in class time. Asking one student to come in ten minutes early and one to stay ten minutes after class is one way to allow for some individual interviews but is more suitable for ongoing assessment than for initial needs analysis, as many class sessions will pass before all the students have been seen.

A third possibility, and the one that is most practical for many multilevel classes, is to present the needs-assessment procedure as the activity for one of the first lessons. The information can be gathered orally, with the teacher acting as recorder and the advanced students offering translation services if appropriate. Alternatively, the teacher may prefer to give the advanced students a more intensive written questionnaire and to work orally with the others on the areas likely to be of greater interest at that level. Initially the students will probably be more responsive if asked to state preferences regarding concrete examples like "Where do you use English more, with strangers or with people you know?" than if asked abstract questions like "What kind of people do you use English with?"

Selection of goals and objectives

Even when the problem of gathering data from the multilevel class has been solved, the question remains of how the needs can be assessed so that goals and objectives can be determined. This is relatively simple for an individual student to do but is extremely difficult when planning for students at different levels, none of whom seem to have the same needs. This is the issue we faced in Chapter 2 when we discussed curriculum for multilevel classes. The solution seems to be to select process goals such as "to use appropriate body language" or "to listen effectively in high-content situations." Such goals do not lend themselves to pass/fail assessment. Rather they lead to intuitive judgments by the students regarding their feelings

of confidence in attempting the process in question and to observational judgments by the teacher regarding the level of difficulty that the students are attempting.

The selection of goals and objectives is the process of syllabus design. While the decision about how to address those objectives will normally be the teacher's, the actual goal setting should involve the learners. As indicated earlier, goal setting is a process at which students improve and get more confident as time goes on. Students who have minimal experience with formal learning will find it difficult to set realistic goals at first, especially if asked the question in very general terms. At this stage, students will usually be happier expressing preferences among possibilities rather than formulating objectives themselves.

Selection of measures of success

Once the students' goals and objectives have been identified, the question arises as to how the achievement of these goals will be measured. Most of us were educated in a system where achievement was measured by some sort of test or examination. At a set time, we were assigned a specific task or series of tasks, and our performance was then compared with the ideal, giving a numerical score. This kind of testing makes it very easy to compare individual students and to identify those who find it easy to produce a set piece of knowledge on demand. It does not tell us whether the individual can produce the language in a real-life situation, nor does it tell us anything about the many aspects of language knowledge that are difficult to measure this this way, such as sociocultural knowledge. One of the main drawbacks to this kind of testing is that, even within its limited sphere of competence, it measures the student's ability at testing time only. This may be acceptable for a foreign-language classroom in which all the students started with zero knowledge, but in a multilevel class in which the students entered the program with widely different abilities, it lacks critical information that the teacher needs about progress. A final disadvantage of assessment tools of this type is the difficulty of developing exams that challenge the advanced students without being incomprehensible to the beginners. Therefore, formal examinations are not a method of assessment that we can use.

The alternative method of evaluating student progress is individual assessment. This should involve both assessment by the teacher and self-assessment by the student.[1] The value of the teacher's informal observation of the students should not be underestimated. As teachers circulate among the students, they should be making notes on a mental checklist, to be written on a more formal checklist later on. These are some of the questions to have in mind:

---

1. One of the reviewers of this book commented that she has had great success with asking students to evaluate each other in a small-group session. She finds that her students are extremely supportive of each other and well able to appreciate the progress displayed. She also adds that a favorable comment from another student seems to have more impact than praise from the teacher.

- Is the student participating to the extent of his or her abilities?
- Is the student interested? Which kinds of activities seem to provoke most interest?
- Does the student seem to grasp the point of activities or require extra explanation regularly?
- Does the student take responsibility when doing a pair task or allow the partner to do the work?
- How well does the student express himself or herself verbally? What improvement has been shown over the last eight to ten classes? Does the student show more confidence in using the same amount of skill? More skill? Or has no noticeable progress been made?
- What does the student's written work look like? Can any progress be seen over the last eight to ten classes? What kind of progress? Greater length of writing? More accurate writing? Wider choice of vocabulary? Better-organized writing? No apparent progress?
- How well does the student respond to oral questions? Can the student understand speech keyed to what the teacher feels is the appropriate level? How appropriate are the responses? Does the student pick up on nonverbal cues? Which is the student better at, getting the general idea of speech or picking out specific bits of information?
- What kind of material can the student read? Is the student challenging herself or himself with material at a slightly higher level or is the student playing safe with very easy material? Can the student cope with high-content material? With tabular material? What strategies does the student use when faced with an unknown word or structure?

The information that the teacher gathers in this way will provide a critical supplement to the self-assessment that the students will perform. While students will be in a better position to assess their progress in those areas where they have made a conscious effort, the teacher is generally in a better position to identify language skills that have been acquired subconsciously or gaps in the students' knowledge that are not being filled. The teacher may notice that certain skills are being neglected, for instance the student's focusing on vocabulary development at the expense of sentence structure. Perhaps certain learning strategies are being overused, as when a student persists in basing reading prediction on the initial consonant of each word without considering context clues. A student may be placing such a high premium on accuracy that he or she spends discussion time preparing one perfect sentence, thus missing the opportunity to develop fluency in argument. These are the kinds of problems that the student is unlikely to recognize and that the teacher must be able to contribute to the overall assessment.

The students' own assessment is another critical component of the overall evaluation. Students themselves know better than the teacher does how confident they feel in attempting something. They can tell you whether the skills they have learned in the classroom work outside in real life, something no examination or test can.

How do we perform self-assessment? Let's acknowledge from the start that it will not be easy for those students who have no oral skills at all; unless interpreters are available, assessment might have to come exclusively from the teacher in the early stages. For other students, however, self-assessment works like this: The teacher draws up an assessment chart or book for each student. Each has a section listing the basic skills, broken down into as much detail as the teacher thinks the students can cope with. Beginners might have just four or five entries, as follows:

- Understand when the teacher speaks to me
- Tell people about myself
- Talk to the other students
- Fill in forms
- Read signs and labels

A more detailed breakdown of the language processes would be provided for more fluent students. Because processes are often expressed in language that is unknown to the students, many teachers prefer to use examples of tasks to exemplify a process. Rather than say "Use scanning skills to identify relevant piece of information," they may, therefore, put "Find telephone number in directory or price in advertisement." Specific goals chosen by the students, such as "write a check," are also listed and, if necessary, broken down further into the component parts of the task: "Write the date," "Write figures in words," and so on. At the beginning of the course, the students sit down individually with the teacher and grade themselves in each area. At different stages throughout the course, perhaps monthly, the process is repeated.

Teachers may wish to record their own comments on the student's chart or may wish for a more detailed assessment than it is feasible to put in front of a student of limited English proficiency. The teacher may also wish to judge overall class progress and may thus feel the need for a way to correlate the information. One way to simplify this procedure is to develop a chart based on fairly broad descriptions of language skills with accompanying sheets defining the various gradings at each level.

With regard to fluency skills, for instance, the chart might be set up as follows:

Student's name_____ Skill group _____

SPEECH SKILLS

	Level 1 grade/date	Level 2 grade/date	Level 3 grade/date	Level 4 grade/date
Fluency				

Key   a. just beginning work at this level

           b. can usually perform at this level in low-stress situations

           c. can perform at this level with ease

Accompanying sheets might define the four levels of the four different skill groups as follows:

Fluency skills

Skill Group One

1. No active vocabulary.
2. Can produce one-word formulaic responses (e.g., good-bye).
3. Can offer greetings, thanks, or other openers.
4. Can answer simple questions on personal matters (name, address, birthdate).

Skill Group Two

1. Can ask simple personal questions of others.
2. Can form simple questions from known or provided vocabulary and has acquired strategies to cope with limited vocabulary.

3. Can understand simple questions or commands and has strategies to cope when fails to understand (e.g., can ask for repetition).
4. Can express everyday needs and make requests (e.g., simple purchases in stores).

Skill Group Three

1. Can understand bulk of what is said by teacher or other trained ESL personnel, asking for repetition or paraphrase if necessary.
2. Can make self understood on nearly all matters to teacher or other ESL trained personnel, with help of strategies such as gesture, paraphrase, and repetition of key words.
3. Can recognize when speech is marked for formality, politeness, or intimacy. Has some control of appropriate forms.
4. Can understand bulk of what is said by native speaker (addressing student) asking for repetition or paraphrase if necessary.

Skill Group Four

1. Can make self understood by native speaker with minimum of repetition or paraphrase. Misunderstandings are more often due to lack of sociocultural understanding than to inaccuracies in speech (e.g. speech gives offense because subject is introduced too abruptly).
2. Can follow conversation between native speakers and recognize hostility, humor, sarcasm, or irony.
3. Expresses self easily without conscious thought. Reacts appropriately to language marked for status or other sociocultural considerations.
4. Operates as a native speaker except for residual accent. Can make self as easily understood in English as in native language, producing language appropriate to situation and role.

With a system like this, the teacher can use the same basic progress chart for each student and has the flexibility to adjust the level specifications to suit the class's abilities. Although this format is suggested for the teacher's comments, there is no reason why such a form cannot be used for student self-assessment if the student has enough language to understand the level specifications, or if the teacher can make this information understood by explanation and examples.

Assessment would be recorded in this way. A beginner student who can offer and respond to greetings and who is just beginning work with simple questions, would assess him or herself against Level One criteria, perhaps completing the form like this:

Student's name _____ *Juan* _____ Skill group _____ *1* _____

SPEECH SKILLS

	Level 1 grade/date	Level 2 grade/date	Level 3 grade/date	Level 4 grade/date
Fluency		*c 3/21/87*	*b 3/21/87*	*a 3/21/87*

Key a. just beginning work at this level
b. can usually perform at this level in low-stress situations
c. can perform at this level with ease

Setting up a system of this type does initially make fairly heavy demands on the teacher but has the useful spin-off effect of forcing us to think hard about exactly what we want our students to achieve and what our definitions of success might be.

A detailed discussion and example of self-assessment is provided in a book written for adult literacy students, *How's It Going?* by Martin Good and John Holmes (Surrey, England: Adult Literacy Unit, 1978). One of the first self-assessment books, it is still one of the best examples of this approach. It is not intended for ESL speakers and consequently focuses exclusively on reading and writing skills. It nonetheless provides excellent practical information about instituting self-assessment. Examples of their self-assessment charts are provided on the following two pages.

Ongoing assessment

Although we have been focusing so far on student evaluation, it is obvious that any modification of the goals or program should also involve evaluation of the teacher and of the materials and approach being used. It is just as critical that we regularly assess our own performance as that we assess the students'. In addition to the ongoing assessment tools that focus on the student, described in the last section, we need tools to help us judge the effectiveness of our own teaching and of the activities we provide.

Reading

TONY

KEY TO SYMBOLS

A = attitude
S = skill
K = knowledge

GRADES

✓ = knows it, is aware of it at this level
O = is working at it, within this level
X = at this level, hasn't started yet

ARROW 1

Do you see reading with a sense of purpose? For real things you need like TV guides, labels, etc., as well as part of getting to learn to read? And without feelings of aversion, even to learn at a go? Can you cope with parts of 'Print First Time', 'Flow Charts' and some newspapers? (We mean can you get the gist of some print, and are your confidence enough to tackle hard print? Can you read on your own? Do you know most of the letter sounds that start words? The necessary ones like 'c' in 'cake' etc.? And can you sound out some words to help you decode the rest? Do you know most of the Social Sight words you need (like 'Danger', 'Exit', 'Entrance', 'Push', etc.)? Can you read without going stuck on words like 'and', 'but', 'the', etc.?

Can you say 'Yes' to most of that? If so, you've 'Not Bad'. If not, you're 'Beginning'.

ARROW 2

Can you read fluently most of the time? Can you tell someone else about what you've read? And give your views on it? Do you know what's available in the library? Can you use reference books? And do you know when to find information, even to have a go? Can you cope with parts of 'Print First Time', 'Flow Charts' and some newspapers? (We mean can you get the gist of some print, and are your confidence enough to tackle hard print? Can you read hard print? If so, can you read for information, DIY books, instructions, official forms, letters, bills, etc.? Can you glance at a newspaper and see what interests you? Then read the bits that you like best of? Do you read for whole because?

Can you say 'Yes' to most of that? If so, you're reading 'With Ease'.

Key	Things to do	BEGINNING						NOT BAD						WITH EASE					
		Date	Grade	Date	Grade	Date	Grade	Date	Grade	Date	Grade	Date	Grade	Date	Grade	Date	Grade	Date	Grade
A	Reading is communication	1/77	X	5/77	✓	11/77	✓	1/78	✓	5/78	✓								
A	Reader's job (Voice)		X		O		✓		O		O								
SK	Alphabet		O		✓														
SK	Social Sight		O		O		✓												
SK	'Key' words		X		O		✓												
ASK	Context cueing		O		O		✓		O		✓								
SK	Visual features		O		O		✓		✓		✓								
SK	Letter names		O		O		✓												
SK	Phonics		O		O		✓		O		O								
ASK	Failure technique		X		✓		✓		✓		O								
AK	Idea of strategy		X		O		✓		✓		✓								
AK	Purposes		X		O		O		X		O								
K	Print 1: L & R		✓		✓		✓												
SK	Print 2: Structure		X		O		✓		O		O								
ASK	Grammatical jargon		X		✓		✓		O		O								
SK	Dictionary		X		O		O		X		O								
ASK	Study skills						✓		X		O								
ASK	Skim/Scan		X		O		✓		X		X								
ASK	Library		X		O		O		X		O								
SK	Speed		X		O		✓		X		O								

(Reading Strategy)

Writing

TONY

KEY TO SYMBOLS

A = attitude
S = skill
K = knowledge

GRADES

✓ = knows it, aware of it at this level
O = is working at it, within this level
X = starting off at this level

ARROW 1

Do you use writing with a sense of purpose? For real things like notes to the milkman or messages, as well as just wanting to learn to write or spell? Do you know about making drafts and correcting them? Can you tell when it's important to spell perfectly and when it's not? Do you write to friends and relatives without worrying? And do you know 'address' and words like 'road', 'street', 'avenue'? Can you fill in easier forms (like Driving Licence Application, Child Benefit Scheme, Giro) on your own? How about cheques? Are you confident about doing these even when others can see you (like in the Post Office or a shop)? Do you have a good way of remembering spellings you want? Can you use simpler dictionaries to check spellings or meanings? Do you have a home-made one? And have you noticed some things about how English spelling works (like the way 'hit' becomes 'hitting')? Do you keep an address book? Are you happy about using full stops and capital letters? Do you ask people how to spell words you're not sure of? And do you sometimes write just for yourself?

Can you say 'Yes' to most of that? If so, you're 'Not Bad'. If not, you're 'Beginning'.

ARROW 2

Do you feel confident about writing whenever you have to? Or want to? Can you fill in hard forms like insurance proposals or job applications without much help? Or ask for help when you need it without feeling embarrassed? Can you use a big dictionary? Do you know quite a lot about how English spelling works? For example, prefixes, suffixes, words with 'ph' in them? Do you feel confident about using commas, semi-colons, paragraphs? Do you keep your papers in a filing system? Can you write formal letters if you have to, like to the Bank, the local authority, the courts? And can you use other styles too, for example in stories or personal letters? Do you sometimes use writing to help sort out your thoughts? If you have to write for your job, can you do it? Or for a course? Without worrying so much that it gets in the way? Can you take useful notes? And is your handwriting fairly readable and fast? Can you often tell when you've made a spelling mistake? Do you feel in charge of it all?

Can you say 'Yes' to most of that? If so, you're writing 'With Ease'

ITEMS			BEGINNING						NOT BAD						WITH EASE					
Key	*Things to do*		*Date*	*Grade*	*Date*	*Grade*	*Date*	*Grade*	*Date*	*Grade*	*Date*	*Grade*	*Date*	*Grade*	*Date*	*Grade*	*Date*	*Grade*	*Date*	*Grade*
A	Writing is communication		9/77	O	1/78	✓	5/78	✓	1/78	✓	5/78	✓								
A	Voice		9/77	✓					5/78	✓										
SK	Form letters		9/77	O	1/78	✓														
SK	Grammatical conventions		9/77	O	1/78	O	5/78	O												
AK	Purposes	Writing Strategy	9/77	O	1/78	O	5/78	O												
AK	Drafts	Writing Strategy	9/77	X	1/78	X	5/78	O												
AS	Editing	Writing Strategy	9/77	X	1/78	X	5/78	O												
ASK	Failure technique	Writing Strategy	9/77	O	1/78	O	5/78	O												
SK	Memorising	Spelling Strategy		O		O		O												
SK	Dictionary	Spelling Strategy		O		O		O												
ASK	Noticing	Spelling Strategy		O		O		O												
AK	Concept of strategy			O		✓		✓												
SK	Writing letters			X		X		O												
AK	Importance of practice			✓		✓		✓												
ASK	Knowing about the language			O		✓		✓												
SK	Note taking			O		✓		✓												
SK	Essays								5/78	O										
ASK	Writing for speech																			
SK	Thesaurus																			

Teacher journals

Most of us were trained to have a lesson-planning notebook in which we write down the activities and resources we intend to use in the lesson. Frequently, though, we abandon our lesson plan for one reason or another. Perhaps a student comes in with some item of interest that sets the whole class off in a different direction. One group may be bored with the planned activity and move on to something else. Another group may spend longer than planned on completing a task, making it impossible to go on to the planned follow-up activity. Many of us routinely plan more than we can do in a day, just to make sure we aren't caught with nothing on hand. This kind of flexibility is one of the marks of a good teacher, and proof that we are responsive to feedback from our students. Over the long term, however, we need to be sure that these changes in plan don't result in an unbalanced program. Perhaps we often plan our lessons so that the livelier interactional activities take place toward the end, when everyone is getting restless with seat work. If we frequently wander away from our set plan, we may find that it is always the same type of activity that is being neglected.

Similarly, activities don't always work out the way we intend them to. We may plan an oral activity, such as finding the differences between two similar pictures, and discover that when the students actually attempt it, they do most of their communicating by pointing and gesturing. Maybe they impose on themselves the writing task of recording their findings, so that a valuable use of time still results, but a different use of time from that planned. This kind of adaptation of activities is particularly common in a multilevel classroom, where a task may be attempted by students with very different skills. Often these adaptations will lead to very useful activities, and we should not feel any necessity for "correcting" the students' performance so long as it does not indicate an over-reliance on one strong skill area and an avoidance of a weaker one.

One of the most useful ongoing-assessment tools we have is to sit down at the end of the class and think about what actually happened compared with what we planned for. In the short term this gives us information about which activities may need adapting before they can be used again. If the information is recorded in a teacher's journal, it allows for an overview of what actually took place in the classroom, thus allowing for much better future planning than the lesson plan book. In the case cited above, for instance, the teacher might want to make two or three changes. It would be a good idea to think back over the directions given with the pictures to see if they were sufficiently clear. If so, and if the pictures are to be used again for oral work, then the method might have to be changed to force oral interaction. Perhaps the students should sit back to back or be asked to describe their findings to another group. Alternatively, the teacher may feel that the students have demonstrated their preferred method of working with the pictures, and therefore plan that the illustrations be given out as a writing task in future. The teacher must also take steps to plan interactive activities for the next lesson to compensate for their exclusion in this one.

Teacher journals are useful for all teachers, but they are a virtual necessity for those with multilevel classes, where it is so difficult to keep track of the varying activities of so many levels of students.

Teacher checklists

With so much to think about in planning activities for students at all levels, it is very easy to overlook certain aspects of an ideal program. This danger can be avoided if you develop a checklist of items that you feel should be incorporated into your class. You won't be able to include everything in every lesson, but a system like this will allow you to tell whether a certain skill or approach is being neglected time after time. The checklist on the following pages was designed for teachers of children and accompanies a unit on science and magic. You might like to use it as starting point for your own checklist.[2]

This checklist is designed to accompany a set of materials that is already well balanced for practice in all the skill areas. The checklist does not therefore provide for an explicit check on balance of skills, a category you would probably want to incorporate in a list for your own use. Some other points related specifically to a multilevel class, which you might want to add, include these:

- Did I allow for some self-selection of activities?
- Did I include some whole-class activities to develop group spirit?
- Did I make clear to the students the purpose of their activities?

2. Sharon Basman, *Teacher's Guide to Abracadabra* (North York, Ontario: Board of Education for the City of North York, 1985).

SCIENCE AND MAGIC

TEACHERS ASK...

Did I Modify the Instructions?

_____ provide visual clues
_____ have concrete materials handy
_____ encourage students to work collaboratively
_____ group students in several ways
_____ demonstrate and discuss the instructions

Did I Help Students with the Language They Need?

_____ step back and observe as much as possible and be an active listener
_____ use facilitative language by restating, expanding and extending when students spoke
_____ give positive feedback
_____ encourage students to
    _____ ask questions
    _____ ask for justification
    _____ persuade others to adopt their opinions
    _____ express emotions
    _____ give explanations, instructions and information
    _____ make hypotheses, predictions
    _____ entertain others
    _____ provide samples of patter
_____ interact with at least 3 students each day
_____ use the tape recorder for student self-evaluation

Did I Help Students Record What They Had Done?

_____ allow for invented spelling
_____ encourage students to write together
_____ give students samples of titles, phrases, vocabulary if they needed them
_____ have students dictate stories
_____ encourage peer discussion before and after writing
_____ have children edit each other's work
_____ suggest drawings as part of record-keeping
_____ promote letters, thank-you notes and other forms of writing in addition to journal writing (e.g., see North York's writing folder ideas)
_____ comment in writing on the content, not only spelling or grammar
_____ maintain interactive journal writing between myself and the students

Did I Assist Students To Expand Their Concepts?

_____ use other resources including the resource librarian
_____ encourage a variety of audiences
_____ incorporate
    _____ music
    _____ drama
    _____ screen education
    _____ research skills
    _____ art

- Did I spend some time with each group of students?
- Did I allow all students an opportunity to play the "teacher" role, at least within a group?
- Did I adjust the grouping arrangements to make sure that stronger students are not dominating the activities?
- Did the students take responsibility for their own learning?

A third useful tool for ongoing assessment is simply to ask the students what they thought of the activities. Students sometimes judge activities harshly when they fail to recognize their purpose. Marian Tyacke, of the University of Toronto, tells of two groups of students whom she asked to assess some language-learning computer software. The first group, which was not given any explicit information about the potential language benefits of the different programs, was unanimous in preferring the formal drill-and-practice type material to the apparently more exciting adventure games. Those in the second group were informed that the drill-and-practice software would provide practice in vocabulary items and structural sentence patterns, while the adventure games would provide practice in reading comprehension, problem-solving strategies, and sentence formation. With this recognition of the potential value of what had formerly been considered mere play, the second group voted unanimously in favor of the adventure games. The lesson for us here is to not expect the students to appreciate the value of activities automatically, particularly those that are unfamiliar, and to make sure that we take the time to explain to our students what it is we are trying to do.

Jean Handscombe, 1985–86 president of TESOL, suggests that a good strategy for getting student feedback and drawing learner attention to the value of certain tasks is to devote the last ten minutes or so of every lesson to a discussion of the day's activities, recorded on a flip chart like a language experience story. Students can be asked not only whether they found an activity useful and what they learned but also why they thought the activity was set up the way it was. This encourages students to think about the learning process and to suggest ways they would prefer to do things.

The final source of information to be used in ongoing assessment is the students' work. If student writing is collected in a folder it should be possible for both teacher and student to see progress made since the beginning of the class. Progress will not necessarily show in more accurate written work; it might be demonstrated in a wider use of vocabulary, more ambitious attempts at sentence structure, more interesting content in written material, or a greater understanding of the needs of the audience. Tapes of oral interaction or monologue will also provide a very useful record. In the first few lessons, students can be asked to make recordings in which they talk about themselves, giving as a minimum their name and address and adding as much information about their background and education as they can. This will give the teacher useful material in the early days when first planning a program, and will also provide an excellent record for comparison with a similar tape made halfway through the course on the same topic. If a videocassette recorder is available, videotapes will give valuable information about nonverbal language uses.

Modification of goals and program
The point of gathering all this information is so that necessary changes can be made. Although the teacher may wish for greater motivation or more effort on the part of the student, in practice the changes will mostly be made to program or teaching performance. Attendance at most adult programs is voluntary, so that learners who show up at all have already demonstrated their motivation and commitment to the program. It may be possible to strengthen motivation by increasing the appeal or relevance of the activities presented, but it is unrealistic to expect students to find long periods of time for homework or to change their lifestyle to mix with English speakers, even though such activities would undoubtedly improve their performance.

In making changes, the teacher should be careful that the cause of any problem is clearly identified. Let's say that group work is unsatisfactory. The required change may not be a decision to drop group work, but a clearer presentation of instructions. Many tasks require a period of adjustment in which the students get used to the new method before they can use the time productively. Before they decide to give up, teachers who are trying new activities should be clear about whether the problem is with the activity itself or with its newness.

Some features we may want to change concern pace, balance, and interest in our activities. Pace refers not only to the amount of time that we allot for a given activity but to the number of exposures to an item that we provide students before we expect mastery. In a multilevel class it is possible for the lowest-level students to be the quickest learners. Let's say that we are working with the beginners on vocabulary for some parts of the body. We introduce the words through a photograph and a game in which word labels are matched with appropriate body parts. Follow-up activities spaced over the next four or five lessons include pair work where one partner asks questions of the other, a bingo game using body parts, and a version of Simon Says in which students touch the appropriate part of the body. If we find by the time we come to the bingo game that all the students have complete control of the vocabulary, we will obviously need to think again about the Simon Says game. Meanwhile we might be doing similar activities with a group that has greater fluency but slower learning speeds, and find to our surprise that these "better" students may need more activities to learn an equivalent amount of vocabulary.

Achieving a balance of the language skills is something we discussed briefly under ongoing assessment, with the example of an activity designed to provide speech practice that turned out to practice something quite different. Balance is more than just a matter of speaking, listening, reading, and writing. Within each major skill area we need to be sure that critical subskills are not being neglected, for example, that all the speech activities do not focus on fluency at the expense of accuracy and pronunciation, or that the listening activities not only train learners in picking out small pieces of content information, but also give practice in assessing tone and listening for the general message.

Few teachers have any trouble identifying problems with interest. We can all see, only too clearly, when students find an activity dull or inappropriate. Student feedback will help us determine exactly which element of the activity needs to be changed. Was the content irrelevant? Was the activity so simple as not to challenge or so difficult as to discourage? Did it call for discussion of a topic on which students felt incapable of commenting? Were the instructions unclear, so that they did not know what the task involved? Some activities simply have to be thrown out, others need only a slight shift in focus to become a valuable part of the program. We can get hints too by looking at those activities that are successful. What was it about them that appealed to the students? Can we introduce that same element into the less successful activities? One word of caution here: Be careful not to overuse certain approaches so that initial enthusiasm gives way to boredom.

Assessing the variety of activities that take place each day in the multilevel classroom is undoubtedly more difficult than for a more homogeneous class. The teacher will no doubt find that what works well with some students is quite inappropriate for others, and that while one student has made rapid progress and fulfilled all his or her objectives, another student, of apparently comparable ability, has made no apparent progress at all. The consolation is that, no matter how variable the rates of progress, there will be activities suitable for the student. Only in a class like this can students truly work at their own pace.

If the student plays a more active role in the learning process, the results will be better for both sides. The teacher will be relieved of some of the burden of assessment, and the students will be able to direct their learning, incorporating preferred style, content, pace, and approach.

4

Classroom Management

Teaching a multilevel class demands that you discard a number of preconceptions. The first one is the idea that everything would be easy if you could only find the right material. Unfortunately there is no right material for the multilevel class—or rather there is a ton of suitable material, but most of it is in your head and the rest is spread out, with a little in each published text. The second idea to go is that all the students should proceed in a lockstep fashion, doing the same activity at the same time. Finally, you discard the notion that a class can be perfect. It is just about impossible to please all the people all the time in an multilevel class, and students have to learn that you cannot always be on call for every little problem.

Although group work is one of the key answers, organizing lots of different group activities can sometimes seem to demand the skills of a juggler or choreographer more than those of an educator. You have to recognize that sometimes things won't work out the way you planned. One group may take a lot longer to catch on than you expected, leaving another group sitting with nothing to do for a while. That's OK. It doesn't mean your lesson was a failure, just that the students haven't yet learned to take responsibility for their own learning. The time won't be wasted, as the students will be getting to know each other and building up a sense of group identity.

Developing group identity in the class
Two features that often go hand in hand with multilevel classes are irregular attendance and relatively infrequent sessions, with the

class meeting perhaps a total of four hours a week. These, combined with open entry and open exit, can slow down the development of a strong group identity. More than most classrooms, the multilevel classroom has the potential for conflict. More advanced students may come to feel that they are wasting their time while the teacher pays attention to the lower-level students. Beginners may feel inadequate in comparison with the stronger students or may resent the fact that one or two strong students seem to dominate classroom activities. These problems will be aggravated if the lines of ability reflect other divisions, such as cultural, political, or age groupings.

The problem will also be aggravated if the teacher organizes the students into two or more permanent groups that operate separately, so that the students form group ties only with those of their own ability. Developing a group feeling within the entire class is always important, but the potential for conflict makes it particularly important in the multilevel setting. For this reason, the teacher would do well first to build up a sense of group feeling within the whole class before breaking the students up into groups and, second, to ensure that a variety of small groupings are used, not merely a rigid split along ability lines.

The choice of activities given to the class or to the cross-ability groups can also help to build a sense of trust and friendship in the class. Any task that must be done cooperatively helps to start the seeds of group feeling. This need not be a complex linguistic exercise. One of the best icebreakers I know is to get the students to rearrange the furniture, a cooperative task that will involve students from all levels of ability. There are linguistic icebreakers that you can use, but sometimes the best task is one that students value as a real-life activity, not just a language game in which they become self-conscious of their linguistic abilities. Asking two students of widely varied ability to fetch a box of books from the staff room is often a more useful task in the long run.

To continue to strengthen these bonds, the teacher will want to develop classroom activities that allow the entire class to work together at least some of the time. Subsequent chapters explain in detail how a start-up activity such as a language experience story can be used for all the learners, even though they will have different follow-up activities. Other activities can use the same stimulus for the whole class but ask for a response at different levels, as for example asking different questions of students listening to the same tape recording. Similarly, examples are given of projects that will involve the whole class, even though students will be contributing at different levels.

Activities such as these will give the students an opportunity to build up a feeling of the whole class as a group, which will encourage the learners to be more at ease and more prepared to try new activities. This is important because group work is one of the main answers to multilevel classes and because it is critical that the students should feel sufficiently at ease to attempt the new behaviors that will be demanded of them.

Students will develop a group identity more quickly if the teacher can relinquish the traditional "leader of the class" role and instead adopt that of advisor and facilitator. This doesn't mean that we never lead a class discussion or tell people it's time to stop work. It does mean, though, that students will often be called on to play the role of teacher, that much more work will be done in groups with students organizing their own leadership roles, and that parts of the lesson will be completely self-access, in which students choose exactly what they want to do without any instruction from the teacher.

Some teachers find it hard to give up the formal role of instructor. It's not really that they like the glory of standing at the front of a class, it's more a matter of not having enough faith in the students' abilities to do things for themselves. Interestingly, it is often the newest teachers who find it hardest to give up the traditional image of the teacher, saying, "My class doesn't like it when I leave them to work by themselves. They like me to tell them what to do." This may be the pattern of education that students are used to, but it does fail to acknowledge their experiences and abilities as adults in charge of their own lives.

Assessing the class

As we have discussed, no ESL class is truly homogeneous, because too many factors affect student progress. Nonetheless, teachers of classes grouped by ability can normally prepare a lesson that will be of benefit to the entire class. It is tempting for the teacher of a multilevel class to try to do the same thing by having ability groupings within the class. Such teachers create their own basic and advanced groups and in effect try to teach two separate classes simultaneously. Unfortunately grouping merely on the basis of basic versus advanced does not take into account the many ways in which students vary. It is better to attempt a more detailed assessment of the students' abilities, bearing in mind that students are often considerably more skilled in one area than another. Some of the critical questions we should ask ourselves include these:

- Does the student have basic literacy skills?
- Does the student have basic oral skills?
- Is the student functionally literate, that is, does he or she have enough literacy to use language-learning activities that presuppose reading and writing ability?
- Does the student have the ability to make himself or herself understood orally? (This may indicate good strategies, rather than a great command of English.)
- Does the student need life-skills or orientation information?
- Does the student wish to focus on accuracy or fluency?
- Does the student have a specific goal in learning English, for example getting a driver's license, or is there a more general wish for an overall improvement in English proficiency?
- How long has the student been studying English?
- How much exposure to English does the student have in daily life?

It is important that the teacher gather this kind of information about the students because the answers will determine both the types of activity that should be presented and the manner of presentation. For example the teacher will need to be aware of those students whose literacy skills are so low that they cannot be given any kind of written task to work on alone or in a group. As well as needing actual literacy teaching, such students will also need the teacher's attention (or that of a more advanced student) to get them started on any written task other than copying. All the other literacy levels represented in the class should be able to attempt group task work based on written instructions, simple though these instructions may have to be for some groups.

Similarly, the teacher should be aware of those students whose listening skills are too weak to follow oral instructions. These students will also need particular attention at the beginning of a new activity to ensure that they understand what they are being asked to do. We might want to pair them with students who can follow directions or who can demonstrate the task at hand. We may want to provide extra instructions for them, helped out with mime or demonstration. At some point we will want to give them activities designed specifically to improve their listening comprehension. We sometimes tend to categorize students by their productive abilities, when for purposes of classroom management it makes more sense to group them by their receptive abilities. Students who understand what is required in a task will find it very challenging if their productive abilities are poor, but they will nonetheless be able to attempt it. Students who fail to understand instructions cannot attempt the task at all.

The other parameters discussed above will affect classroom planning in similar ways. Students who can make themselves understood orally will be able to attempt oral activities, such as a problem-solving task, on their own. The fact that they make themselves understood by a clever use of such strategies as gesturing, repeating themselves, and falling back on a word from their native language will not affect their ability to communicate. They can thus hold their own with students of far greater fluency and accuracy.

Some of the questions above are designed not so much for classroom management as for selection of activities. Those students who need orientation information might wish to practice their reading on authentic material like school reports, health fliers, and telephone books. Students who want to focus on accuracy might benefit from a lesson on an item such as question formation, with the weakest students trying to commit a single question form to memory while stronger students work with different levels of formality or politeness.

It can be seen, therefore, that the students should not be categorized simply as strong or weak, but rather by their strengths and weaknesses in particular areas and by their needs and interests.

Using smaller groups

It is amazing how quickly even the most rigid students adapt to new techniques if they are introduced gradually with clear explanations of what is expected, and if the students have had a chance to get to know the group. One of the basics of group dynamics is that it is much easier to change the behavior of a group than of an individual. People are more prepared to try new behaviors in a group; within a very short time group members wish to identify with the group leaders and will make great efforts to do so.

There are also a number of pedagogical advantages of small-group work that the multilevel teacher can exploit.

- In a large class generally only one person can be speaking at a time. Small groups provide students with many more opportunities to try out their oral language. The less confident students can also get useful practice before a mixed audience, which is not as intimidating as an entire class.

- Small groups can attempt problem-solving techniques, which will call on a range of skills other than linguistic ones and will give each student a chance to contribute.

- Small groups can more easily be geared to the particular interests of the learners. One group may be discussing hockey while another talks politics and a third works on a grammar point.

- Small groups allow for different learning styles, as they give learners the chance to explore in the direction they want at the speed or the degree of depth they want.

- Small groups can be used to make good use of teacher aides or visitors to provide genuine conversation or a chance for quieter students to cross-question and elicit information at their own speed.

- Small groups make it possible for students to work with realia of various sorts (timetables, bills, newspapers, fliers, letters) in cases where it would be impossible to get enough material for the entire class.

All these advantages make small-group work a method of choice even in homogeneous classes. In a multilevel class it is a virtual necessity. Some small-group activities will be best performed by groups in which the language abilities are as near to equal as we can arrange. Other groups will benefit from a deliberate mix of abilities. In other cases the best groups may be those that students select themselves, presumably groupings of friends or those sharing a common interest.

When students of differing ability are grouped together, the critical factor is most likely to be personality. A dominant student who is also an advanced learner will try to take control of the group if no counterbalance is provided. Generally speaking, it is better to put all the strong personalities together and let them slog it out, and to put all the quiet ones together where they will be forced to verbalize their concerns.

Group size

Avoid the temptation of splitting the class into groups determined more by their numbers than by the ability of the students. The logical division of a class of eighteen students may appear to be nine and nine, but in truth may be more like three and fifteen because of the ability spread.

The size of a small group can vary considerably, depending on the task at hand. In classes that have students in two or three clear ability groups, the teacher will sometimes want to split the students on these lines, setting up tasks that will occupy most of the groups without their needing help, freeing the teacher to spend time with those who need it. If the task is one that students do individually or in pairs, the size of the group is unimportant. The teacher is not really using groups in the sense of interactive units; rather, two or three different classes are operating at once. True group work is designed to make the members of the group interact and communicate with each other. The goal is for students to participate in a conversation, to swap information back and forth, to share knowledge, and to argue out strategies.

The optimum number for a group like this is between three and seven. It is generally held that an odd number of students is best, so that stalemates can be avoided in discussion situations, but I find this a problem only in activities that demand that the group reach a consensus. Seven is considered to be the absolute maximum for a single conversation, and three is really a little low, as a single dissenting student is likely to give way rather than take on the remaining pair. Therefore five is generally considered the optimum number for most activities.

Fixed groups

Leaving aside the question of numbers, should you have fixed groups or divide the class differently in different situations? Fixed groups have some advantages, the main one being that one can save a lot of time in getting groups organized and started on a task. In my experience, however, the delay factor is only really critical when the class is first being shown how to work in groups. The first time any new activity is presented, the students will spend more time learning how to go about the activity than they will actually spend doing it. This does not mean that the time is wasted. There is a great investment for future lessons, which will settle down remarkably smoothly once students have grown used to the kind of thing you expect.

While they are struggling to understand you and your instructions, the students are having an excellent opportunity to acquire English with a focus on content rather than form (assuming you are not teaching in a bilingual class, in which case instructions shouldn't give you much trouble, anyway). They are also probably interacting as a group, even if only to mutter, "What is the teacher up to now?" Fixed groups get to know each other quickly and build a strong sense of group identity. For new students they provide a protected

environment in which to try out new material.

The main disadvantage of fixed groups is that patterns of dominance and leadership tend to develop within the group. Quieter students have less incentive to make an effort, and the rest of the group may feel a responsibility for lower-level students and, with misguided concern, carry them through the activities without their ever making an attempt to function alone. Some of this can be overcome by making it clear to the class that group activities are just that. While help should always be offered to group members, the students need to make the effort to contribute, or they are wasting their time. Some personality conflicts are not so easy to settle, however, and a quicker solution is to reorganize the groups.

Another problem with fixed groups comes when the numbers fluctuate or irregular attendance destroys the personality balance in a group. If students have grown used to always working in set groups they tend to resist reforming to suit the needs of a particular occasion.

Multiple groups

The compromise position is to have a number of different group combinations with which the students are familiar, so that they regard themselves as belonging to one of three or four different combinations. The absolute minimum arrangement is to have equal-ability and cross-ability groups organized. (You may want to set these up on both oral and spoken parameters, according to the activity). The quickest way to plan these groups is to rank the students roughly in order of ability and lay the numbers out in a matrix like this one, where 1 represents the lowest-ability student and 16 the highest.

	red	yellow	green	blue
A	1	2	3	4
B	5	6	7	8
C	9	10	11	12
D	13	14	15	16

A layout like this allows the teacher to ask quickly for the students to assemble by letter for groups of approximately equal ability or to assemble by color for cross-ability groupings. It also provides a perfect matrix for jigsaw activities, in which individual group members share information they gathered in another group (see Chapter 6 for details).

The teacher might also draw up bigger groups based on literacy skills, or special groups for discussion, in which personality is likely to play an important role. A flexible arrangement of groups also allows a student to split off and work on his or her own.

Overcoming resistance

Teachers should be aware that classes that have never worked in groups may display some resistance to the idea at first. Because the first trial of a group activity demands so much learning of routines and determining of expectations, the planned language activity may not happen very satisfactorily. Minimal success, combined with the apparent lack of student enthusiasm, has led many teachers to give up at this point. With every apparent justification, they point out the right of the students to select their own learning style. This is a valid concern, but it ignores that the teacher also has an important role in the teaching-learning process and that there are times when the teacher knows better than the student what will be successful. If teachers are aware that student resistance to grouping is common but normally short-lived, they will be more prepared to give it a fair trial.

Encouraging student responsibility

Students in a multilevel class cannot be given the luxury of sitting back quietly and letting the teacher carry the burden of responsibility for them. If they decide to coast along without making an effort to learn, the teacher will merely assume that their skills were not as advanced as at first supposed. There is no standard of comparison for the progress made by the multilevel student. Evaluation of progress can only compare with the student's previous work. In a multilevel class the students must come to realize that new behaviors will be demanded of them. They will be asked to get up out of their chairs and work at different stations. They will be asked to work with students of different abilities. They will be asked to

EFFECTIVE CLASSROOM MANAGEMENT

perform tasks that can only be completed with an exchange of information. They will be asked to solve problems.

Students who expect to sit in the same seat next to the same partner, writing exercises from the same book, can find these demands really disconcerting. But the newest innovation for most, by far, is that the students will be asked to decide for themselves what they want to learn and how hard they want to work at it. Many tasks that students can work at provide a rich opportunity for language use if carried out in the suggested fashion. If students choose to communicate the information in their native language or ask a more advanced student for all the answers, however, nothing will stop them except their own recognition that their presence in the class is their own choice and that the responsibility for learning rests with them. The teacher is wise to avoid more than an occasional reminder of the rules, rather than trying to take on the role of police officer and provide external discipline. Students have to make their own decisions to learn. Often students will work out their own solutions to problems if the teacher can hold back long enough from interfering.

As later chapters of this book point out, many activities are available to a multilevel class. Some of them require the whole class to work at the same task, others have everyone doing different aspects of the same process. There are activities for equal-ability groups, for cross-ability groups, for pairs, and for individuals. Wise teachers will not rely exclusively on any one pattern but will call on all of them, according to which is best for the skill being practiced. In many cases the choice of activity will lie with the student.

5
Activities for the Whole Class

As we discussed in Chapter 4, although small-group work is a staple in the multilevel classroom, it is still important that the whole class work together on some activities. The kinds of activities that can be done by an entire multilevel class can be placed in three major groups: 1) start-up introductory activities that are usually followed by group work, 2) activities in which members of the class apparently are working on the same task but in fact are performing at different levels of complexity, 3) whole-group projects in which everyone will interact but will perform different tasks.

Start-up activities

Many teachers like to have all the students work together at the beginning of the lesson. This plan allows for some discussion of what is going to happen that day, provides an opportunity to dispose of any housekeeping tasks such as registration, and gives the teacher a chance to set the tone for the day.

The usefulness of having some social chat at the beginning of the lesson should not be underestimated. The actual language used in greeting students, asking about their health and that of their families, commenting on a new outfit or hairstyle, and so on may not be understood by the lower-level students but will nonetheless give them useful exposure to normal conversational interaction. In our enthusiasm for useful, realistic interactions that exchange information, we sometimes forget one point: often conversation is not used to exchange information at all. Rather it is intended simply to main-

tain the ties of friendship, express our interest and concern, and re-
assure ourselves that our conversational partner is still sympatheti-
cally inclined to us. This is the reason that when we are asked "How
are you?" we answer "Fine" even when we feel pretty awful. We recognize that the question is not truely an inquiry about our health.

Students may not appreciate the importance of this kind of communication. Their neighbors and colleagues may perceive them as
being reserved if they communicate only when they have information to express. The multilevel class gives an excellent opportunity
for those who have strong speaking and listening skills to practice
this kind of conversation while simultaneously providing a model
for the less advanced students. Students should be encouraged to
interact rather than having the conversation limited to the teacher
and individual learners.

Most start-up activities suitable for the whole class involve a lot of oral language development. It really doesn't matter that the lowest-level students will only pick up some of what is being said. The young child acquiring her first language only understands half of what her mother says to her, too. The way she learns the other half is by being exposed to it. Students will follow the conversation at the level of which they are capable and will focus on those items that they feel capable of learning, so long as the discussion or activity does not become so abstract that they lose sight of what it is about and start to tune out. If the teacher and advanced students begin a discussion of the government's financial policy, most of the class will tune out immediately. The easiest way to be sure the conversation keeps a concrete referent is to have some visual input that gives a handle on which to hook language comprehension. Some of the best ideas are described below. It should be borne in mind that these suggestions are only intended to start up an activity. Numerous suggestions for follow-up activities are provided in the section on group work.

Filmstrip, video clip, or film
If you show a visual without the sound track the first time, the students become aware of how much they can predict from context, manner, body language, and action. This is as true for the beginners as for the advanced. Depending on the example chosen, there may be some ambiguity as to the exact story line, and students can be asked to guess at exactly what they think happened. Because this calls on cognitive skills rather than linguistic ones, all the students have an even chance of being right. It is impressive how hard lower-level students will struggle to express themselves in such a situation, whereas in tasks depending more on language ability they will tend to give way to the more fluent students.

A short film or film strip can be usefully shown at least three times to a multilevel class without risk of boring them. After the first silent viewing and the ensuing discussion about the amount that it was possible to deduct without any help from the language, there can be a second showing with sound so that the students can check the accuracy of their predictions. The teacher will also want to use the visual to develop vocabulary and to demonstrate useful phrases or particular speech patterns. On a third showing, the visual can be interrupted so that questions can be asked on the lines of "What's that she's holding? What do you think he's going to say next? Who's this? Is that his car? What's her job? How would you describe this woman?" It is easy with this kind of questioning to adapt the questions to the level of the student, thus allowing for success at all levels. Lower-level students can get yes/no questions ("Is that a hat in his hand? Are they married? Is she angry?") accompanied by gestures and mime if necessary. Advanced students can be asked "What do you think he's saying? Why is she standing like that? Why is he so upset? What do you think the relationship is between these people? Why?"

Film strips have the advantage that the teacher or students can control the rate of progress, which allows for images to be pointed out and for students to try to patch together a possible dialogue to accompany a frame. Films and videos provide a more realistic example of language use and give a better chance to explore body language and other sociocultural aspects. If the teacher has access to a good-quality video player that allows for slow motion and freeze frame, video can provide the best of both worlds.

Field trip

Field trips provide an excellent opportunity for experiences shared by the whole class and involve lots of language use at all levels. Although long-distance trips to places of historic or cultural interest can be fun, field trips don't need to be so adventurous. Often having the whole class go out to the nearest coffee shop that provides waitress service, so that the students can place their own orders, turns out to be highly successful. Visits to such local facilities as the library, the emergency department of the hospital, the fire station, or the post office can prove to be very interesting too and can make students realize that these services are more easily accessible than they thought. A visit to a class member with a new baby or to a hospitalized fellow student is another valuable trip. Useful sociocultural information is likely to come out in the discussion beforehand regarding the appropriateness of the visit, the best time to go, and the acceptability of various gifts.

Language experience story

The Language Experience Approach, or LEA, as it is often called, is one of the most valuable techniques available for low-level ESL

learners. Although it is less commonly used with higher levels, it can in fact be valuable there too, so long as challenging follow-up activities are provided. LEA deserves more explanation than there is space for here, and teachers unfamiliar with it are urged to read some of the books recommended at the end of this chapter. Briefly, in LEA the class as a whole discusses a starter topic, which may be a shared experience like a field trip, a recent event that has affected everybody, such as a major holiday, or a visual stimulus in the form of a large clear photograph or picture such as the one shown here.

In the discussion phase, vocabulary is raised, and students can try out ways to describe their feelings or observations. Then the teacher asks for contributions to a class story and transcribes the story provided by the students onto the blackboard or a large sheet of paper, reading aloud the contributions as they are transcribed. Students thus have a reading text relevant to their own experience that is expressed in familiar vocabulary and uses structures they have produced themselves. The task of reading becomes much easier for the students, making it comparable to that facing a native speaker. The story might take a form like this one, which was in-spired by the picture shown.

Faming

There is a granafather reading a book. mat ther is cooking a lunch. grand mather is feeding baby. father is bathing in the bathroom.

baby sleeping in the crib

In a multilevel class the level of text contributed by the students will reflect their varied abilities. The teacher can compensate for that by soliciting contributions from the lowest-level learners first. Their sentences will thus be up for view longer and will be read aloud many more times, as the teacher always starts reading from the be-ginning of the text when reading the text back to the students with the addition of a new sentence. Higher-level students are unlikely to be challenged reading the sentences that the lower-level students are capable of forming, but their attention can be maintained if they are warned that later they will be asked to spell the words presented on the board, to correct any grammar mistakes recorded (and the teacher records exactly what the students say, mistakes and all), or to join the simple sentences presented by the beginners into com-plex ones.

LEA provides for a wide variety of follow-up activities. Beginner students will work only with the first four or five sentences of the story, ideally the sentences they themselves have created, trying to recognize key words or read back the story. A correct but simple sentence, perhaps contributed by one of the better students, can provide a model for pattern practice if each word is written out on a card with spare cards for substituting alternates. Other students can work on a cloze version of the text or write their own stories from scratch.

Demonstration

A practical demonstration of a skill or craft can provide an opportunity for language acquisition for all class members and can act as the starting point for work on content or form. The students will have skills of their own, or a visitor might be persuaded to come in and demonstrate first aid, palm reading, wood carving, cake decorating, playing a musical instrument, or the basics of car maintenance. Much more prosaic things can also start off a class. The workings of the video machine or projector can make a useful demonstration (in addition to encouraging students to take charge of such equipment in the classroom in future). All such events should involve the students as much as possible. Actually doing something is the best way to make sense of the instructions, and a demonstration should always end with a hands-on attempt where possible.

Interview questionnaires

These provide practice in all the skill areas, with an excellent opportunity for all class members to interact. Students are asked to interview every member of the class (including the teacher) and discover some item of information. This can relate to any topic, preferably one under discussion. Do you come to school by bus? When is your birthday? How many sisters do you have? Do you like eggs? might all be possible questions. Students record the responses on work sheets that list the names of all class members, as in the example shown on the following page.

In a multilevel class more than one question should be provided, but students should be asked to get a complete set of responses to the first question before beginning on the second or third. This increases the number of interactions and ensures that higher-level students do not confine their interaction to asking three or four questions of other fluent speakers, rather than giving all students a chance to respond. The first question should be very easy, preferably answerable by yes or no, thus minimizing the burden on the lowest-level students. Second questions might be on the lines of "How often..." or "Where do you...", thus requiring one-word an-

Can you swim?

Can you ride a bike?

Can you fly an airplane?

	Swim	Ride a bike	Fly an airplane
Irene	*yes*	*yes*	*no*
Magda			
Larissa			
Denzel			
Fazli			
Jill			
Kirsten			
Thalia			
Karen			
Ida			
Sung			
Hui Leng			
Norati			

swers. Other questions can be as difficult as the teacher feels the class can manage, as only strong students will get through the previous questions quickly enough to attempt them.

If the spread of abilities is very wide, a second section can be provided on the sheet for students to attempt only if they complete the main exercise. For a class working with the question "What did you do yesterday evening?" the further task could consist of manipulating the data in some way, for example, "Which students stayed home? What was the most popular activity?" and so on. Alternatively the original questions could be extended to include people outside the classroom—secretaries, other teachers, janitors, and so on, which is a very useful opportunity for contact with native speakers.

Once the beginners have completed the first question, the class can come together to tabulate the results on the blackboard. This provides material for further work with identifying and comparing.

Map reading and development

Map literacy does not seem to be directly related to the other literacy skills, so students may show surprising amounts of skill (or lack thereof) in this field. Draw up a small map of the immediate area with letters or numbers to identify key places such as the school, supermarket, plaza, and park. Give each student a copy, and discuss together the identity of the marked places. Rather than drawing the map so that the school is placed centrally, place it at one edge of the map so that only the area to one side of the school is illustrated. Ask the students to contribute to a map on the board that shows the area on the other side.

If it is possible to get multiple copies of highway maps, the class can work together following a route described orally by the teacher, trying to be first to identify the town reached at the end of the journey. Students can take turns choosing a place and giving directions to reach it, with low-level students giving their directions as a series of highway numbers written on the board if they prefer. All the students proceed to asking for and giving directions, with low-level students concentrating on a key phrase like "Where is....?" and higher-level students working on clear oral and written directions.

Maps of the world are also fun with a multilevel class. One of the things we should exploit fully in ESL classes is the fact that all our students are travellers with experience of at least two cultures. A map can be an easy way to lead into this. Have the students identify their home country, perhaps with a colored pin or small flag. Have them draw the route they took to reach North America, marking all the places they stopped on the way. Colored thread can be used if you prefer not to draw on the map. Charts can be made of the number who came from a certain place, or who stopped at a particular city. Students can quiz each other about the location of places, coming up to the map to select a place and picking the student who will answer the challenge. Students who select difficult places can be made to give clues such as hemisphere, continent, and country. Students can thus choose for themselves how difficult they wish to make their task.

Family photos and snapshots

Showing family photos always seems to work best if the teacher brings in a pile of her or his pictures first, especially if some of them

are fairly candid. Old pictures that show the teacher as a teenager are often a great icebreaker, and wedding photos are bound to arouse interest, especially if the wedding was some years ago and fashions have changed. There is a cultural element to sharing photographs, and some of your students may be a little reluctant to bring in pictures. You will also want to be extremely careful if any of your students are refugees who may have lost family members. In most classes, however, learners enjoy the chance to find out a bit more about each other and cheerfully show off pictures of their children and other relatives. An enjoyable activity is to get the class to attempt to match photographs with their owner. This can be done with old photos of the students as youngsters, or it can be done with pictures of the students' children to see if there is a family likeness.

Cartoon-strip stories

A number of ESL books around now provide picture sequences. Some of these are funny or tell a little tale, others are straightforward descriptions of everyday life.[1] Both sorts make a useful starter activity, with students offering vocabulary items or complex sentences about what is taking place. The story can be used later for tasks as simple as sequencing the cut-up frames or matching one-word captions to the appropriate pictures, or as complex as writing a newspaper article of the event portrayed.

Photo stories

Students of all levels can follow photo stories with balloon or caption dialogue if they use the clues contained in the illustrations to help them figure out the meaning. Listening to stronger students read out the dialogue gives poorer readers a chance to hear it before attempting it for themselves.

---

1. L.A. Hill, *Picture Composition Book* (London: Longman, 1960). The shading and style of these pictures makes them more suitable for use with literate students than with those who are unaccustomed to print conventions. Each set of pictures tells a story.

   J. Dumicich (consultant), *Picture It: Sequences for Conversation* (New York: Regents Publishing Co., 1978). Clear, simple pictures describing everyday routines, such as getting up.

   L. Mrowicki and P. Furnborough, *A New Start: Students' Book* (Exeter, N.H.: Heinemann Educational Books, 1982). Although not exclusively a picture book, this course book includes some excellent picture sequences of daily routines.

Tasks with cognitive demands

While the teacher will not want to focus too frequently on cognitive skills that are not directly related to language use, an occasional game that allows for success without language skill can be a useful opportunity for all students to have a fair chance at excelling. Kim's Game is a test of memory in which students look for one minute at a tray with some twenty objects on it. The tray is then removed and the students list as many items as they can remember. Items can be drawn if the English word for them cannot be remembered, but the English vocabulary will be thoroughly reviewed when the results are checked. Similar games can be played regarding the order of arrangement of certain items, which can be chosen for their vocabulary relevance. Sometimes items from intelligence tests, such as the relationship between a sequence of numbers, will be of interest.

Follow-up work to these activities will need to provide students with an opportunity to focus on the specific skill of which they are in most need. These starters, though, can provide an example of natural communication together with an opportunity for the entire class to interact together and thus develop the kind of group spirit that will make all members feel more comfortable in the class.

Tasks for the whole class, performed at different levels

A second major way in which all the members of a multilevel class can work together is to use exercises and activities in which a single source of information can produce different responses. While such tasks as listening and reading essentially are done individually, it is not always practical to make different reading or listening matter available for all the ability levels. If the class is working with a theme, it is useful if everyone can work with the same piece of material. With listening material this is often essential simply because of problems with equipment and noise levels.

The difficulty level of an exercise is often determined less by the complexity of the input than by the task. All learners, for example, can listen to a conversation between native speakers and get something out of it. Even zero-level students will benefit from exposure to the sound system of English and be able to hazard a guess whether the interaction is friendly or hostile, formal or informal. They could perhaps listen for one or two key words and judge whether the conversation is about children or business. Stronger students can get a general idea of the drift of the conversation and perhaps be able to identify that one speaker is asking the other for some information. More fluent students should be able to follow the same conversation and identify the details such as what, where, why, and when. They should be able to assess the relationship between the two speakers, and determine whether sarcasm or irony is being employed.

The amount of information brought to the task also relates to its difficulty. In general, the more a listener or reader knows what to expect from the source material, the easier he or she will find it to process. The teacher can thus reduce the demands on lower-level students by ensuring that they have clear ideas as to what will be required of them. This could take the form of providing a couple of simple oral questions, to which they must identify the answers, or a partial description of the material at hand, which they must complete.

By using different techniques like these to adjust the level of difficulty, a single source of input can be very useful in the multilevel class. The source material can be auditory or visual.

Tape
A tape recording can take many forms. Genuine native-speaker conversation, complete with interruptions, hesitancies, and unfin-

ished sentences, is often one of the most difficult listening tasks, aggravated by the fact that recordings of really spontaneous conversation are not made in sound studios and thus tend to be poor in sound quality. While valuable, they are better used in smaller groups where earphones can help to offset some of the distortion. Students can be urged to listen in to native-speaker conversations on the bus and in stores and restaurants, where they will have the added advantage of visual clues to help them guess at what is being said.

I find semi-authentic conversation to be more useful for multi-level learners. I get two native speakers in a quiet room with a tape recorder set up, brief one of them on the general drift of what I want said but leave the other to respond naturally. The conversation is then recorded without any rehearsal. This maintains natural speech rhythms and spontaneous expression, but avoids the rambling quality of completely unscripted conversation. It also enables tapes to be relevant to the theme or topic at hand.

Another way to get material is to record from the radio. A brief item from a news broadcast or a weather report might provide practice with high-content material. A clip from a phone-in radio show will provide a more conversational format, although care must be taken that the sound quality is good enough for classroom use. A song with discernible lyrics could be useful, as could some of the more interesting commercials. Students can also be asked to call a prerecorded telephone message and be given a list of things to listen for.

Recordings of dialogues can be useful too, so long as they are sufficiently realistic and rich in interactional terms to challenge the advanced students. This need not be a matter of length or complexity of sentence structure, as is shown in a comparison of the following two fragments.

A I saw you were talking to Mrs. Smith at the meeting. Is she still having trouble with those figures that we were discussing last week?

B Well, I think she got it sorted out once the corrected printout came back from the computer. She didn't seem to think that there would be any more problems.

A You were talking to Mrs. Smith. What's the problem now?

B   Oh, still those figures.

A   Aren't they sorted out yet?

B   Oh yes, I think so.

A   Well, what was wrong this time?

B   She needed the corrected printout. I think it's sorted out now.

A   Let's hope so.

The second dialogue is much simpler than the first in structural terms, but much more complex in interactional terms. Even without the added information that could be given to the second dialogue by intonation and stress, we can already read between the lines to recognize speaker A as being more powerful than speaker B, to see that this is not the first time that Mrs. Smith has had problems, and to acknowledge speaker A's exasperation. Dialogues of this sort lend themselves more easily to work with students of different levels, as information is presented both factually and inferentially.

Material of this sort can be assigned together with any of these tasks that seem relevant to the needs of the class:

- Listen to the tape while following a transcript.
- Circle any of these words you hear on the tape (provide ten words, five of which appear in the conversation, five of which do not).
- Complete a cloze transcript of the tape. Demand could be as minimal as three or four words known as sight vocabulary by literacy students (e.g., the, yes, he) or could be random deletion of every tenth word, every verb, or every function word.
- Yes/no comprehension questions on simple factual matters.
- Yes/no/don't know comprehension questions. (These demand greater skill as students must decide whether the information required is provided on the tape. This reduces guessing based on matching a single key word in the question.)
- Comprehension questions that demand lengthier answers (who, where, what, and—especially—why)
- Comprehension questions that require inferences to be drawn from the text (e.g., Is this the first time Mrs. Smith has had a problem? How do you know?).

Activities for the Whole Class

For tapes that contain a lot of factual information, students can be asked to take notes or complete a matrix. Imagine a conversation between a customer and a sales clerk, in which the customer is trying to decide on a gift and considers a number of different items, all of which are on sale. One student could be given the following small chart to complete, with the task being merely to jot down the amounts as they are mentioned.

Item	Regular Price	Sale Price
Tie		
Gloves		
Red Scarf		
Blue Scarf		

Other students might be asked to take notes with no guidance provided, so that they must impose order on the information they are hearing as well as record it—a much more difficult task. For an easier task, a student would be given the chart with the information already complete, but with one or two errors that must be identified. The student can then concentrate entirely on listening without the distraction of simultaneously attempting to record information.

Reading passage

Reading passages can take as many forms as the tapes. Sometimes the reading will actually be a piece of continuous prose, perhaps taken from an ESL text or specially written by the teacher to incorporate certain language features, but other useful reading tasks can reflect real life. A bus timetable, a notice of real estate tax assessment, an airline ticket, a child's school report, a notice about an upcoming meeting, an advertising flier, or a completed application form will provide material that can be usefully studied at all levels. Human-interest articles from the newspaper, cartoon strips, and letters are also useful. All these forms of reading material have the advantage of format and layout that help even beginning readers make some predictions as to the likely meaning of the text. Pictures, headings, titles, figures, and names can all give valuable clues that are missing in a straightforward piece of prose.

The variation in tasks can include the following:

- answering comprehension questions of varying degrees of difficulty, as outlined above for listening
- completing a missing word in a given sentence by matching it to the text
- copying key sentences (highlighted in students' copies)
- responding to the text, e.g., writing a reply to a letter, completing a check form for the appropriate amount of a bill, completing the comment section on a child's report

Materials for skimming or scanning

The lavishly illustrated advertising fliers put out by the big department stores are ideal for these exercises, as it is usually fairly easy to get enough of them for a class set. Travel brochures, timetables, and health pamphlets are also suitable if you can find sufficient copies.

Ask students to find different things according to their level. Lowest-level students can be asked to find the price of certain clearly identifiable items, such as the red coat, a pair of men's work boots, etc. If they have no oral English, the items in question can be provided in pictorial form from another cut-up copy of the flier. Stronger students can be asked to find out if the men's boots are waterproof, or whether the red coat is available in size twenty. If necessary they can be given fliers from two competing stores and asked to identify which has the best deal on a specific item with certain required features. Students should be encouraged to work quickly on this task, as it is designed to reduce the dependency on reading every word. As well as reading quickly to locate specific pieces of information, learners should get practice in sampling the text to get a general sense of the content. This task, best done with newspapers, can also be assigned at different levels. Just recognizing a sports story from a financial one is an exercise in skimming. Slightly stronger readers could assess horoscopes as being lucky or unlucky, while good readers scan the entire paper for the articles on specified topics, for example those related to health.

SPELLING BEE

Team games

If the class is divided up with an equal spread of abilities, team games can be played with questions adapted to the level of the learner. Spelling bees are an obvious example, as the word assigned can be chosen specifically to be within the learner's competence.

The teacher can also even out the balance in other games of this type. Variations on the "What am I/Who am I?" idea, in which one student chooses a person or object and the other has to guess, can be made much easier for beginners if suggestions for key questions are on the blackboard. As well as the format "Are you male or female? Are you alive or dead?" questions can also be put up in the form of a pattern table, as in this example:

Is	he	in	sports?
	she		politics?
			entertainment?
		from	the Philippines?
			Vietnam?

97

Other team games might look for the first team to match vocabulary cards of something like body parts successfully to a large diagram, with easy terms being assigned to beginning students. Alternatively, the team could label the parts with the proviso that every member must write at least one word, even if the word is provided by a stronger team member.[2]

Dictation

This also can be done at different levels if only the most advanced students actually attempt true dictation and the others do cloze tasks of various degrees of difficulty. The sentence

The woman got on the bus and sat down.

could be transcribed in full by good students. Others might be given

The _____ got on the bus and _____ down.

or,

The woman _ ot on the bus and _ at down.

Similarly, spelling tests might be given; the stronger students begin with a blank sheet, but weaker students are asked to circle the correct spelling from a choice of two.

Activities for the whole group that incorporate different tasks

A third way to allow the class to work together while still providing useful learning experiences for all members is to attempt projects that involve a variety of tasks. For example, the class could regularly issue a newspaper, which could be photocopied or simply pinned up on a bulletin board. The first useful task would be the organizational phase, which will provide excellent acquisition opportunities for all students as they decide on the different tasks involved and parcel out responsibilities. The students will often do better here if the teacher allows them to organize things in their own way and does not try to impose too much control. Some of the tasks that

2. A good source of ideas for language games is J. Steinberg, *Games ESL People Play* (Toronto: Dominie Press, 1985).

could be attempted are these:

- Stronger students might write articles based on rewrites from published newspapers, interviews with native speakers (in person or by telephone), or information researched from resources provided by the teacher or identified by the individual student. They could also work out lists of questions that moderate-ability students could use as guides for interviews. They could take final responsibility for proofreading for accuracy of grammar and spelling.
- Medium-level tasks include writing up horoscopes or creating letters and responses for a lonely-hearts column. If these tasks are attempted in small groups they will provide opportunities for oral work, negotiation over choice of content, and editing each other's work, thus providing feedback on clarity of writing style as well as accuracy with language.
- Students with minimal literacy skills could practice their sentence-structure patterns by writing single-sentence captions for photographs. Checking headlines demands the ability to recognize content words, while writing them out neatly at a suitable size from handwritten copy provides good letter-formation practice. Arranging layout demands the ability to scan articles to ensure that the appropriate headline is attached and that the article is arranged in the right section of the newspaper.

Another project that students can attempt as a class is the production of a photostory. The students themselves take a series of photographs and briefly caption them to tell a story of common interest. The story might grow out of a language experience story that was developed in class, or it might reflect an experience of particular interest that one class member has related to the class. Ideally, though, it will be a series of photos that involve all members of the class, thus ensuring interest. Some of the best sources are class field trips or class parties at which a photographic record is made. The class can then get together to view the photographs, decide which ones should be included, and organize the sequence—a discussion activity with a clear visual base that should allow all students to participate. Students can then decide for themselves how they want to arrange the photostory. Perhaps they want to pin the photos on a bulletin board with typed captions underneath. Maybe they prefer to glue them on a large sheet of white paper and write the captions underneath. They may decide to work in pairs, with each pair responsible for captioning three or four photos, or they may prefer to have one team do all the draft writing, another check it for accuracy, and a third copy it neatly onto the finished story.

More ambitious, but useful because of the wide variety of language tasks involved, is the creation of a slide tape show. Students in one multilevel class I worked with decided that they wanted to produce something that looked more professional than a wallboard display and decided to attempt a slide tape. Collaboratively they wrote a simple story line based on a social event that they could all attend, which provided roles for all the class members. One group then worked on setting up plans for the actual filming, identifying a site and filming date, drawing maps of the location, and arranging for the burden of providing refreshments to be shared. Another group took responsibility for props and interviewed all other class members to check their contributions against a master list of what was required. One group worked on the lettering for the credits, with title frames, lists of actors, etc. The final group drew up a list of the various frames that they felt had to be shot to illustrate the story they had in mind.

Shooting went according to schedule, and the students impatiently awaited the return of their photographs so that they could select the best shots. With the slides projected onto the screen, everyone was able to join in on deciding which shots were clearest and most satisfactory. There were some failures, of course, and discussion ensued as to ways of getting around the problem. Sometimes the problem could be solved by adapting the story line a little or by inserting a spare slide from another sequence, as for example when a farewell slide was substituted for an unsatisfactory arrival sequence.

When everyone had agreed on the final selection, the next stage was the recording of the sound track. The photographs had been taken only on the basis of a story board; now the actual script had to be written. The students opted to work in pairs and write the dialogue for one or two frames each; this demanded a lot of interaction to make sure that the dialogue flowed smoothly without too many repetitions or non sequiturs. With the final selection made as to which students would read which parts (with everyone being on tape at least to the extent of offering a greeting to the hostess), the dialogue was recorded frame by frame, with the click of the stop button functioning as the frame-advance signal for the visual. The finished product was extremely impressive and one that the students took a good deal of pride in showing off at the end-of-term party.

The project's linguistic benefits were even more impressive. A very mixed class had an opportunity to work collaboratively. The students got practice in listening, speaking, reading, and writing. They worked on pronunciation, map literacy, problem solving, and negotiation strategies. The students got out of the classroom and used their English in a social, conversational setting. They had contact with native speakers (purchase of supplies, negotiation with administration over petty cash, invitations to school personnel to attend final screening, etc). Some of the weakest students had an opportunity to be stars, as the faces for the major roles were provided by the lowest-level students with dubbed voices coming from the more fluent. Similarly, the photographer and sound engineer, also beginner students, were both women who had never touched cameras or tape recorders before but learned their skills on the job.

Students sometimes underestimate the value of the linguistic opportunities provided by projects of this type, and measure only the tasks with a visible end product, such as the creation of a line of dialogue. If the teacher is going to make use of these opportunities for students to work collaboratively and to acquire as well as to learn, it is important that the benefits should be pointed out to the learners. They are less likely to fall back on their native language or to get by with the bare minimum of English if they are conscious of how useful the interaction phases are. The teacher must also be prepared to acknowledge the value of letting the students be responsible for all phases of the project and resist the temptation to do much of the organizing.

Here are some other project tasks suitable for mixed classes:
- Planning an "invite a guest to class" session. This can involve invitations, maps, planning for refreshments, putting up signs around the building to point guests in the right direction, interacting with the administration to assure their cooperation with outsiders on school premises, plans for entertainment, provision of name tags, etc.

- Planning a field trip. Tasks would include phoning or writing to places of interest to request brochures and information, summarizing and comparing information received (perhaps in tabular form), discussing amongst the group the merits of various locations and location selection, writing to make arrangements, inquiring about transportation and making necessary arrangements, calculating costs, writing notices to remind students who may have missed planning sessions, making arrangements for a photographic record, drawing a map of the route, and so on.

- Putting on an entertainment of some sort for another ESL class, children in a local school, patients in a local hospital, or residents in a home for the elderly. Tasks would include most of those described above for the slide tape show, plus valuable contact with native speakers in finding out what the potential audience would enjoy, making the necessary arrangements, interacting with the audience after the show, and possibly writing follow-up letters. An entertainment such as a Christmas party for deprived children involves students in the further tasks of writing gift tags, invitations, letters from Santa, and instructions for games, while interaction with the children would provide plenty of native-speaker contact in a low-stress situation.

Useful Further Reading

Dixon, Carol N., and Denise Nessel. 1983. *Language experience approach to reading (and writing): LEA for ESL.* Hayward, California: Alemany Press.

Asher, J.J. 1977. *Learning another language through actions.* Los Gatos, California: Sky Oaks Productions.

Nessel, D.D., and M.B. Jones. 1981. *The language experience approach to reading: A handbook for teachers.* New York: Teachers College Press.

Stauffer, R.G. 1980. *The language experience approach to the teaching of reading.* New York: Harper and Row.

6
Group Activities

In Chapter 4 we discussed the many advantages of group work, both for the students and for the teacher, and considered some of the ways that learners in a multilevel class could usefully be grouped. In deciding the composition of a group, the teacher should bear in mind both the needs of the students and the activity being planned. Before examining the special needs of the multilevel class, we should consider the following general parameters regarding group work:

- The smaller the groups, the more people can be talking simultaneously in the classroom. Pairs of students thus theoretically provide the greatest chance for verbalization, but in practice this is only true for dialogues and other set pieces of text where the students are practicing speaking rather than talking. Conversation and discussion are likely to be more successful with a small group. In addition, if the students need to practice such skills as persuasion, negotiation, interruption, and turn taking, a small group of three to five will provide more opportunities.

- Small groups will not automatically produce lively conversation and interaction if they are merely told to discuss. Rather, the task itself must demand the interaction, by requiring students to get information from each other or to reach a consensus position by persuading each other. The goal should always be a clear end product that cannot be achieved without interaction.

- Listening activities can be done in groups of any size from two up, but a larger group requires less talking and more listening. Students will also get practice with separating the speaker from background noises if they are listening in a group situation rather than in pairs.
- Odd-numbered groups do well in problem-solving exercises, avoiding an impasse. Groups of seven or more tend to break into two separate conversations and are best avoided.
- Group work should not be based simply on reading. When ESL students are asked to read text aloud, they tend to focus their attention on decoding the sounds and achieving correct pronunciation rather than on getting the meaning of the text. Unless you intend the activity to be a pronunciation exercise, reading is better assigned as an individual activity or as one component of group work so that, for instance, students are assigned a piece of text to read and must then report back to the group on their findings. If your students enjoy reading aloud chorally or singing from a text, make sure they have a chance to read the material for meaning first.
- Although writing is often thought of as an individual activity, it can be performed collaboratively very well. Writing in a group can provide immediate feedback, and editing and can develop the sense of writing for an audience. One successful route is for students each to write a piece (which may be as short as one line for beginners), which is then read to the group for feedback, followed by revision. Alternatively, the group can work on a joint product, writing a line or paragraph each for a shared story.
- Grouping arrangements will affect the interaction patterns in a classroom. Whereas small groups of four or five students favor student-to-student interaction and provide a useful forum for individual interests, larger groups favor interaction between student and teacher.

In addition to these general parameters, some special points should be borne in mind when using groups in a multilevel class:

- Dividing a class into two or three fairly large groups is useful when the teacher knows that one section of the class will need a considerable amount of attention and guidance before a task can be begun. By setting the other students up with a task that will keep them occupied, the teacher is able to concentrate attention on those who need it.

- Activities that develop accuracy work best with equal-ability groups, in which the focus of the activity is more likely to be relevant to all students. Activities that develop fluency work well with multilevel groups, because the stronger students can provide a model for the weaker ones yet can be challenged themselves by the demands of restating and clarifying their speech to make it comprehensible even to a basic-level student.

- Advanced students can make excellent tutors for beginners and can still be challenged themselves in the process. Rather than always using a one-on-one arrangement, however, a valuable plan is to have two advanced students help one beginner. This forces the two advanced learners to discuss the source of the beginner's difficulty and increases their own understanding of how the language works.

- Group activities can be set up so that every member of the group must give input (e.g., each person has a picture to describe) or in a format in which less confident students can sit silently if they want (e.g., discussion). Absolute beginners will often welcome the chance to be able to follow an activity without the stress of being called upon to produce anything themselves and will be happier with the second type of activity. After a while, however, they may be ready to produce English themselves and resent it if the more fluent students dominate the discussion. They will then be happier with activities that give everybody a chance to participate.

- Collaborative writing is also useful for beginning writers. A useful strategy for literacy students is to free them from some of the demands of the writing process. If one student writes and another dictates, one has responsibility for spelling, punctuation, and letter formation, while the other focuses on content, vocabulary, and structure. Alternatively, the various demands can be shared, as students decide together on correct phrasing or spelling. This kind of freedom is excellent when the group is composed of students of equal ability.

- When students vary widely in ability, the teacher will want to select tasks in which definite roles are imposed, ensuring that the more advanced students do not take responsibility for all aspects of the process. The student with weaker literacy skills might be assigned the composing process and the more advanced student given the transcription. Using a comic strip as a starter, for example, the beginner might be assigned a description of two of the frames (particularly those where the provided dialogue would be helpful). The more advanced student would be given the task not merely of describing the other frames but of "writing around" the beginner, that is, modifying his or her own text to avoid repetition of the partner's contribution and providing any neglected requisite information.

Equal-ability groupings

The term equal-ability grouping can be a little misleading, as it is used to refer to different grouping patterns, one of large groups, one of small.

In the first sense, a teacher may find it easier to teach a multilevel class by splitting the students into two groups, each of which does different work. As an extreme, the teacher may have two sets of textbooks, each with its own syllabus, and may organize activities so that while one group is working from the text, the other group has the teacher's attention and vice versa. In effect the teacher is teaching two smaller classes rather than really using group work. Although it is to be hoped that no teacher would permanently split up a class in this way, sometimes this kind of broad ability grouping makes it possible to spend intensive time demonstrating and explaining to one group an item that may be quite irrelevant to the other. The lower-level students may, for instance, all benefit from a lesson on completing checks and bank slips, a task that more advanced students may fulfill on a daily basis. The more advanced students might want to discuss family roles in North America, an abstract topic that would be impossible for the lower-level students to follow because of the high linguistic demands. Any activity that can be done with a whole class can be done with ability groups of this sort. The real challenge comes in devising satisfactory activities that the other group will be able to work on without needing constant checking, encouragement, or intervention from the teacher.

Group Activities

The other meaning of the term equal-ability grouping refers to setting up small groups of students who have approximately equal skills and who will attempt to work together on a task. In such a set-up there may well be two or three groups of learners at a given level; that is, if the class has nine beginner students, they will break up into two or three smaller groups for activities of this type. They are, therefore, grouped in this way not merely to solve the problem of the multilevel class, but because some useful activities can only be done in small groups. Moreover, the very use of the small-group strategy allows the teacher to set up the classroom so that students can attempt tasks suitable for their level rather than having to work at the level of the majority. Because most small-group work is self-directed, it also frees the teacher to circulate among all the groups, providing help and guidance where required, or to work intensively with one group, such as literacy students or citizenship candidates, who may need some special attention.

The major types of activity suitable for this grouping by student ability are those relating to problem solving, sequencing, and process writing.

Problem solving

Students are presented with information that gives them a number of choices. They are asked to record their decisions individually first and then to discuss their respective conclusions and reach a group decision by consensus. The situations presented can be very close to everyday life or can be set in fantasy. An entertaining example of the latter, intended for advanced learners, puts the students in the situation of having crash-landed on the dark side of the moon. They can only carry five items with them and must decide on the relative merits of objects such as flares, water bottles, matches, solar reflectors, and so on. General knowledge, such as being aware that matches would not light on the airless moon, helps students persuade others to their point of view.

Enjoyable though such a task might be, many students prefer something closer to home. Good use can be made of advertising fliers as a source of the basic information that students can use in making a decision. The fliers from a supermarket might be given with instructions that read, "Some very special guests are unexpectedly coming to dinner, catching you with empty cupboards and only \$20 in your wallet. Use the food ads for prices and design the best, most balanced meal you can come up with." Alternatively, advertisements from clothing stores could be used to select the best outfit for a specific occasion, using a limited budget, or fliers from a building center could be used to design the best way to give a face lift to a beaten-up recreation room or studio apartment.

Problem solving need not involve the spending of cash, of course, although these exercises tend to be the easiest way to present material that can be used even by students of fairly limited reading ability. For better readers, choices could concern lifestyles. They could select the best career option for a young immigrant, matching the "situations vacant" advertisements of the newspaper with a description of the person's talents and experience, or they could try to identify the best accommodation for a family also using the classified ads. They could discuss four or five possible courses of action for a woman who is concerned about her aging parents now living alone in the home country. They could decide on a course of action for a young woman being sexually harassed at work or a young man who suspects his boss of dishonesty. In all these cases, the provision of four or five reasonable choices will usually provoke more discussion than merely posing the problem, in which case students may go along with the first one to come up with a sensible suggestion.[1]

A real-life problem that relates to the students' own interests is an excellent choice. Jean Unda[2] describes the valuable discussion that took place in her workplace class over a payroll problem one of the workers was experiencing. Discussing the worker's possible ways to handle the problem had a reality that strengthened everyone's interest as well as providing valuable information.

Sequencing
Material that breaks down into a series of parts works very well with a small group. The individual parts of a written or illustrated story are given to members of the group, who must share their informa-

---

1. Some commercially available materials using this approach are these:
B. Bowers and J. Godfrey, *Decisions* (Toronto: Dominie Press, 1983).
B. Bowers and J. Godfrey, *Decisions, Decisions* (Toronto: Dominie Press, 1985).
D.R.H. Byrd and I. Clemente-Cabetas, *React Interact* (New York: Regents Publishing Co., 1980).
2. See J. Unda, "An approach to language and orientation," *TESL Talk*, 11 (1980): 4 (Ontario: Ministry of Culture and Recreation).

tion with each other to reconstruct the original. A number of activities can be assigned that depend on whether the students want to work on their oral or written skills.

Some activities use pictures as a foundation:

- The students are each given one picture from a story sequence, which they do not allow the others to see. They take turns describing their pictures, questioning each other for further details if they are not clear. After all the pictures have been described, the group tries to identify the correct order of the pictures from the verbal descriptions. All the students then show their pictures to see if the supposition is correct.

- Pictures are given out as above. Each student writes a sentence on a slip of paper to describe his or her picture. The sentences are then arranged to make a story.

- Pictures are arranged face up in random order on the table. One student is appointed as the one to arrange the sequence, but she or he can only move pictures on the instructions of the others. All the others must keep their hands behind their backs so that they verbalize their commands and do not use gestures.

- Each student is assigned one picture and writes a sentence or two describing it. Sentences and pictures are then placed randomly on the table, and students attempt to match caption with picture. Alternatively, the story and sentences can be exchanged with another group for matching.

- One picture is removed from the sequence before the students see it. Students study the pictures and decide the likely location and content of the missing picture. Collaboratively they write one or two sentences describing the picture before turning it up to check the accuracy of their prediction.

Other activities are based on a print story:

- Students are each given a sentence, which they must memorize. They then tell their sentence to the group, which decides as a whole on the correct order. When they are satisfied that they have the order correct, they recite the story for the teacher or check it against a written master copy.

- Students read their sentence two or three times before the slips are collected. Then they try to write down the sentence as best they can on another slip of paper. The new sentences are then arranged in sequence and checked against the master copy.

- Students are each given a sentence to memorize or paraphrase. One student has a sentence that does not belong in the story at all. Each student recites her or his sentence and the group decides which is the unnecessary sentence. This activity can be made suitable for very advanced students if the extra sentence is detectable by style rather than content.
- Sentences are given out as above but a key sentence is withheld. Students try to decide on the location and meaning of the missing sentence.

Process writing

For a long time in ESL we have focused on what our students produce in writing rather than looking at the process by which they have produced it. Too many writing exercises have been of the type that required the student to write out complete-sentence answers to carefully staged questions. In teaching writing this way we have failed dismally to help students improve their writing skills.

Students whose writing is weak in any language need to develop the ability to make a clear statement and to support it with examples or details. They need to develop a sense of what the audience will bring to the reading, so that they neither assume knowledge on the part of the reader that is lacking, nor provide information that the reader will know. ESL learners who are skilled writers in their own language will be able to transfer many of their skills, but they still need practice with English style. They may write in a style that is considered weak, wordy, or flowery in English, or they may organize their arguments in a manner that seems strange to the English-speaking reader, for instance, presenting a wealth of supporting material before stating the basic premise. To improve our students' writing we need to focus on the process by which they write and to provide feedback so that they can revise.

The process is as follows: Students work in a small writing group. They discuss ideas for writing topics (including some possibilities suggested by the teacher) and offer inspiration to each other, but each student chooses her or his own subject. They are encouraged not to feel that they have to write a "story" with a beginning, middle, and end, although many students seem to prefer to start with some sort of narrative. Often students find it easiest to begin by relating their own experiences. They might describe a childhood memory, their wedding day, or a problem at work. Others may prefer to write about a movie they enjoyed or describe what is happening in their favorite soap opera. As they become more fluent, they will develop the confidence to tackle writing in which the order is not determined by chronological events. They may follow up a problem-solving discussion by writing out their argument, or they may want to express a long-standing irritation with their landlord or some institutional organization. Often students who have a real-life writing task facing them, such as a business letter, will appreciate the chance to draft it in class and get feedback.

When a student has completed a first draft (and this could be done at home if the student wishes), he or she calls for a critique by one or more students from the group. The author reads the draft aloud, and the audience is asked for suggestions. Often the very task of reading aloud makes it clear to the writer when critical information is missing. Feedback comes in the form of "I didn't understand that bit. Which man are you talking about?" "Say that sentence again; I didn't follow it." "This sentence is good, but that one is too long." By criticizing others' work, the writer develops a sense of what is required in good writing.

If the students are in groups of approximately equal ability, the feedback is likely to be at a level that is valuable for the writer. Beginners will tend to focus on the word-choice level or on the provision of required information. More advanced students may need feedback that shows them how to order information logically or provide cohesion and coherence in a passage. This will often come from the teacher, who will take advantage of the critiques to present explicit suggestions at a level suitable for the group's abilities. The teacher's feedback is important to the process, but as it will not be possible for the teacher to be available for all the critiques, the suggestions and comments may sometimes be given individually or in written form.

Students can edit their work as many times as they wish. The writing will be made public only when the writer is pleased with it. This "publication" could mean inclusion in a class bulletin, pinning the work up on the wall, or inclusion in a small booklet of class writing.

Cross-ability groupings

Cross-ability groups can serve to strengthen fluency skills if they are properly planned. Lower-level students will be exposed to much richer language than they will meet in equal-ability groups, and stronger students will be challenged to restate their contributions in order to make them understandable by the beginners. This is only true if the task is sufficiently well organized that participation from all levels of students is a critical part of the task, however (with the exception, as mentioned earlier, that absolute beginners should not be forced into productive roles with which they are uneasy).

Discussion

Discussion activities tend to be dominated by the more vocal students to the point that the others tune out, but tasks that can be done cooperatively are excellent for mixed-level groups. For example a small group might decide to "publish" a recipe book of their favorite ethnic recipes. Such a project incorporates a number of tasks, such as interviewing classmates and staff for contributions, researching other cookbooks for ideas on format, selecting a layout style, adapting contributed recipes to standard format, copying recipes neatly

onto ditto or master for photocopying, grouping recipes by type, and putting titles in alphabetical order for an index. As can be seen, some of these tasks are extremely complex, others fairly easy. Mixed-level pairs might work together to do the interviewing, with one student presenting prepared questions and the other recording the answers. A project like this, in which the tasks are very specific, ensures that the beginner students will play a critical role and not be overwhelmed by the superior language performance of the other students.

Board games

Another activity that allows different levels of students to interact usefully is the use of teacher-made board games. The element of luck in such games helps offset the importance of language skill, and it is fairly easy to handicap advanced players in some way to make the game more challenging.

The simplest sort of game is a "trail" game, in which students roll dice to determine how many spaces they can move along the trail. As they hit certain squares, they are called upon to perform certain language tasks. One simple version of this that I codeveloped is designed to teach banking skills.[3] Squares along the trail were color coded alternately to represent deposit or withdrawal transactions, except for a number of squares bearing instructions like "Go back four spaces." A stack of laminated deposit and withdrawal slips was provided, which had to be completed according to instructions, then compared with the correct sample provided on the reverse. Students progress along the trail, rolling the dice and completing the slips. The wild-card squares help slow the advanced students down a little, as does the practice of allowing beginners to roll two dice rather than one, thus halving the required number of transactions to reach the end of the game.

The Monopoly format also lends itself to simple language games, perhaps with players purchasing pieces of clothing to make an outfit or food items to make a meal, the winner being the first one decently covered or nutritionally balanced. Another interesting variant, developed at the British Council in London, is a trail board with pictures of different items in each square. Players are given a

---

3. J. Bell and K. Weinstein, *Banking* (North York, Ontario: ESL Modules Project, North York Board of Education, 1980).

set of cards describing people for whom they must buy gifts. Each time they land on a square they must attempt to explain to the other players why the pictured item would be an ideal gift for one of their assigned characters. Only if they can come up with a convincing rationale are they allowed to cross that character off their shopping list. Adapting this game to multilevel groups could be done simply by giving a shorter shopping list to less fluent speakers, or by assigning the difficult characters to the more advanced students.[4]

Jigsaw groupings

Another way of putting students into mixed-level groupings and ensuring that they all have a critical contribution to the task is jigsaw grouping. In this method students are placed initially in equal-ability groups. Each group is given some information unknown to the rest of the class. They are then rearranged into new mixed-level groups, each new group being made up of one student from each of the original groups. The learners then pool their knowledge to attempt some task that can only be completed if all students contribute. Most commonly the class is broken into four groups of approximately four students each, as 16 seems to be about the average number of students. Much smaller classes would do better with three groups, while large ones might need to make five. Unless one or two students are left over, it is better to have one small group for which the teacher can summarize missing information at the appropriate level than it is to have overly large groups in which some students will never be called on to participate.

Jigsaw activities can be used with either listening or reading as the source of input, or a teacher could develop an activity based on researching information.

An example of a listening jigsaw might go as follows: The teacher makes four tape recordings of family conversations. Each conversation features the weekend plans of one family member. The lowest group gets an easy-to-follow tape of a mother talking on the phone to a rather deaf grandparent, where every remark is repeated two or three times. The second group hears the father discussing his plans with a colleague. The next group hears a teenage child discussing an upcoming school dance with a friend. The top group

4. A good source of ideas for games is F. Klippel, *Keep Talking* (Cambridge: Cambridge Handbooks for Language Teachers, Cambridge University Press, 1984).

hears an adult daughter being pressured to go out on a date and presenting excuses. Each ability group listens to its tape and discusses the content. According to level, they may be assigned comprehension activities or be given some other task such as roleplay or assessing the language for attitude clues. When the equal-ability groups are confident about the material, the teacher rearranges them into cross-ability sets made up of one student from each of the original groups. Each student in turn tells the group the gist of the conversation he or she heard. The students are then given a simple chart to complete as follows:

	Saturday			Sunday		
	Morning	Afternoon	Evening	Morning	Afternoon	Evening
Mother						
Father						
Teenager						
Daughter						

Jigsaws for reading and writing follow a similar pattern. In this case the input comes from reading material adjusted to the different levels of the students. They may, for instance, read three or four different accounts of the same event given by people who all were involved. A human-rights incident, for example, might produce the following four texts of increasing difficulty: 1) a personal letter from victim, 2) a brief newspaper account, 3) a formal statement to a human-rights commission from a perpetrator, and 4) an investigator's report.

Other ways that the teacher can divide the input between the ability levels include breaking a story up into four chronological parts and writing each part at a suitable level or presenting four different ethnic holidays or four ways of celebrating the same holiday.[5]

---

5. Commercially available material that uses this method is E. Coelho, *Duplikits: Jigsaw Activities for Multilevel Classes* (Toronto: Duplikits, 1985).

7
Pair Work

The major advantage of pair work is that it gives each student the greatest opportunity for verbal interaction. Theoretically, 50 percent of the class can be speaking at any one time, each with the immediate feedback and critical attention of an audience. Not only do students get the chance to verbalize, but also this chance comes in what is presumably the lowest-stress setting of all—an audience of only one, and that one another student who is well aware of the problems the speaker faces in attempting to articulate.

Working in pairs is not only for oral communication activities. Any task that students might attempt individually can become more useful and more communicative if attempted with a partner. A grouping of two is small enough to allow for collaboration on grammar exercises or written work. Students can check each other's pronunciation or test each other on vocabulary. Even a reading task can be done collaboratively, with the pair comparing notes on their understanding of what they read, or with the task divided so that each reads half of the text silently and reports the content to the other.

Another advantage to pair work in the multilevel class is the ease and speed with which activities can be initiated, enabling a profitable use of short periods of time that would not allow for the greater organization required for successful groups. There are, though, some limitations on the use of pairs, most of which concern the dynamics of the pair relationship. If students generally work with the same partners, one student will likely begin to assume a dominant role and take the major responsibility for getting the task accom-

plished. Weaker partners will be inclined to give way when dis-
agreement arises rather than argue their position, which they might
in a group discussion in which support is available. A situation can
arise in which one partner is doing all the work and thus most of
the learning. The likelihood of this presumably is greater when the
students are of different ability levels to begin with. To offset these
potential problems, the teacher needs to take care both with pairing
arrangements and task design. If students always work with the
same partner, breaking up a pair with personality conflicts will be
difficult. Depending on the task, the teacher might want to encourage pairs of equal ability or partnerships where stronger students
are paired with weaker ones. In either case, sufficient flexibility
should be maintained so that students do not always work with the

same partner.

The task can also be adapted to suit the nature of the grouping. Rather than allowing for free discussion, which one student can dominate, the task should be one that can be performed only if both parties contribute, for example a roleplay. The weaker student's contribution may be minimal but should nonetheless be critical. Examples of tasks that demand participation from both students are provided below.

Equal-ability pairs

Using pairs in the mixed-level class makes it clear that language knowledge is only one factor in a students' progress and preferred approach to learning. Three or four pairs of students of apparently similar ability will produce very different results when assigned the same task. The speed of work will vary. The focus will change, with some students working rapidly toward completing the task and others preferring to go more carefully. Some will want to discuss the process, with frequent questions like "Is that how you say it? Did I say that right?" Others will focus only on the content and the completion of the task. Some will use dictionaries to check any unknown words and pause to record the new vocabulary in their personal dictionaries. Others will guess at new items or use other strategies to avoid troublesome areas. Learners working in this way are not merely working at their own level but also at their own pace and in their preferred learning style. This kind of flexibility is not so easy to achieve in larger group settings and can be one of the greatest boons of pair work.

The actual activities assigned to the pairs can vary widely, depending on the focus of the day's lesson. In addition to the communicative ideas suggested below, many more traditional activities, such as testing mastery of structural patterns or vocabulary, can well be adapted to pair work.

Information gaps

For these exercises, both students of a pair are given information on a certain topic. Each student's account has some information blanked out, and students must discover the missing information by asking their partner. This activity is adaptable to all levels of student. For beginning students, the task might be set up like this:

Student A		Student B	
Penguin Cleaners		**Penguin Cleaners**	
PRICE LIST		**PRICE LIST**	
Suit	____	Suit	6.95
Coat	5.95	____	5.95
____	4.50	Jacket	4.50
Pants	2.50	Pants	____
Skirt	____	Skirt	3.00
Dress	5.00	____	5.00

The same activity can be made more challenging for advanced students if the two students get their information in a different form. The change might be as simple as rearranging the order of items for one partner so that they must search the entire text for the answer rather than merely proceeding point by point. For more advanced students the actual source of information might differ. One might get a police report of an incident and another a private letter written by the victim describing what happened. One might get a transcript of a telephone call between a passenger and an airline while the other gets a copy of the airline timetable. Articles on the same topic from two different newspapers will usually provide sufficient overlap of information that gaps blanked out of one can be answered by a search of the other.

Puzzles and games
Another way to encourage students to exchange information is to develop a set of small games and puzzles that demand description of the items before the task can be completed.[1] One version of this involves pairs of cards with pictures of items (each pair of cards is identified by color or by a number or letter on the back). Each student takes one card of a pair and holds it so that the other cannot see the picture. The students then describe the picture they are holding and decide whether they have the same picture.

---

1. A number of good books include suggestions for language games. See the resources section at the end of this book.

Pair Work

For all levels about 20 percent of the cards should be identical. For beginners the remaining sets should be clearly different, one picture of a house, one picture of a dog, etc. For more advanced students, the pictures should get more and more similar, thus demanding more description. There might be pictures of two red coats, one with a collar, one without, or pictures of two different men, both with mustaches and curly hair. This will demand very detailed descriptions of the pictures if the learners are to be sure that there will not be any surprise differences when the pictures are turned face up.

A similar game involves having one partner arrange items into a pattern specified by the other. This requires duplicate pictures cut into standard sizes or glued to cards of standard size (3" x 5" index cards cut in half make a good standard). Pictures cut from advertising fliers are useful sources here. Each pair of students gets two sets of identical pieces. One partner arranges them into a square or rectangular pattern, out of sight of the partner. The partner then has to try to recreate the arrangement by following the verbal instructions of the first student. For low-level students, give out only six to nine pictures per set and make sure all pictures are clearly distinguishable. For more advanced students, give out sixteen or twenty pictures, and choose items that are similar so as to force more detailed description. The task also becomes more difficult if the student trying to recreate the arrangement has more pictures than are necessary. The pictures can be used repeatedly and with mixed-ability pairings, however they are time-consuming to prepare. Once the students are familiar with the format and use of the pictures, you may wish to bring in a pile of raw materials one day and ask each of the students to make a pair of pictures for you. The organization and sharing of tools and equipment will no doubt involve considerable language use as well as relieving you of a lengthy task.

Another puzzle version involves pictures with deliberate mistakes that the students must spot, or pictures such as those in *Look Again Pictures*,[2] in which two versions of a picture are presented, with some eight or nine minor differences that the students must spot. These pictures are detailed and, for most students, too complicated for differences to be identified merely on the basis of lis-

2. Judy Winn-Bell Olsen, *Look Again Pictures* (Hayward, California: Alemany Press, 1985).

tening to a partner's verbal description. Rather, the students should look at both pictures and make a written list of differences.

Dialogues and roleplays

The terms dialogue and roleplay seem to be open to a number of interpretations. It might be useful to define them for the sake of clarity.

The term *dialogue* refers to a scripted conversation between two or more people that students are asked to read aloud after hearing it on tape or read by the teacher. The dialogue usually incorporates certain language features on which the teacher is focusing and provides the students with a chance to see them in use. Students may eventually learn the words of the dialogue and recite them from memory, occasionally even substituting words into the set phrases. They do not, however, essentially change the format of the dialogue or contribute to it.

In *roleplay*, the students are given a situation and called upon to create their own conversation. The situation may be a familiar one, with students playing themselves, such as asking each other for change or borrowing a stamp. More commonly, one learner maintains the student role while the other acts the part of store clerk, telephone operator, or other native speaker with whom students must interact. Many teachers are reluctant to attempt roleplays in which both parts lie outside the students' experience, arguing that such situations can have little relevance to the students' needs. Others feel that games and drama provide a welcome opportunity for learners to try out language while freed from the embarrassment of putting their own personalities on display. This choice depends on the individual class.

Reading dialogues aloud is a traditional way in which teachers make use of pairs. It provides students with a chance to have controlled practice of a structure within a meaningful context, especially basic-level students who do not have sufficient fluency to create phrases of their own. Dialogues are limited in that they can be adequately performed without any understanding of the meaning of what is being said. Unlike real speech, in which we must listen to our conversational partner's response before we can formulate our next speech, in a dialogue we know exactly what our partner will say and consequently are not called upon to listen. If students are capable of creating their own lines, they should always be asked to roleplay rather than to read a scripted dialogue. Lower-level students may not have that ability and will need the support of a printed script, at least as a base for improvisation. Dialogues can be made much more useful for such students if an element of compulsory listening is incorporated into them. The simplest way to do this is to provide speakers with a choice of lines. They must select the response that is applicable to their partner's comment, but they are still relieved of the burden of creating a sentence themselves. In this example, student A begins with the query in the first box and student B can choose either response from the second box. A must listen sufficiently to decide which of the responses in the third box is appropriate.

A	B
Are you going to the plaza for lunch?	Yes. Do you want to come? or No. I'm going to the cafeteria.
Sure. What time are you going? Oh, I don't like the cafeteria food.	Well, it's cheap. or One o' clock. See you by the front door.

At a slightly more advanced level, the selection of appropriate items might be determined by suitability as well as meaning. A formal greeting might be followed by a choice of responses, only one of which would be at the appropriate degree of formality and intimacy.

Good morning, Mrs. Jones.	Hey, how you doing? or Good morning or Hi, Fred

Although reading dialogues can be made more meaningful in this way, roleplays still provide a better opportunity for students to practice formulating their own utterances. Unlike dialogues, which must be written in advance and adapted to the different students' abilities, roleplays will be adapted by the students themselves. Roleplays must be grounded in work previously covered and provide an opportunity for students to try out the new language that they have been working with receptively. Roleplays will thus often grow out of prepared dialogues that may have been presented on tape, or as part of a filmstrip or video. In the multilevel class this is very useful. While the lower-level students will be challenged just trying to read aloud or remember the first few lines of the prepared dialogue, the stronger students can be working more creatively. A simple dialogue like this phone call to a beauty parlor to make an appointment might provide the spin-off activities that follow.

A   *Good morning. Hair Waves.*
B   *Oh, hello. This is Mrs. Lee. I'd like to make an appointment, please.*
A   *One moment please. Who do you you usually see, Mrs. Lee?*
B   *I haven't been to your salon before.*
A   *Oh, I see. OK, what did you want done?*
B   *Just a trim and a blow dry.*
A   *Uh-huh. When did you want to come in?*
B   *Do you have anything on Saturday morning?*
A   *This Saturday? No, no. I'm afraid we don't. Not in the morning. Saturday's rather a busy day for us. Could you come in at 2:30? Susie is free then. She could do you.*

B   *Two-thirty? Oh, well, I suppose so. Oh, OK.*
A   *It was Mrs. Lee, wasn't it? I'll put you down for 2:30 on Saturday then?*
B   *OK. Thanks.*
A   *OK, Mrs. Lee. Good-bye.*
B   *Bye.*

Level 1: Work with the greeting and identification phrases, substituting their own names. After reading the lines aloud a few times, they attempt to say them without help. Repeat procedure with farewell sequences if time allows.

Level 2: The students are given the following reduced dialogue. They read it aloud four times, twice in each role.

A   *Good morning. Hair Waves.*
B   *Oh, hello. This is Mrs. Lee. I'd like to make an appointment, please.*
A   *Oh I see. OK, what did you want done?*
B   *Just a trim and a blow dry.*
A   *Uh-huh. When did you want to come in?*
B   *Do you have anything on Saturday?*
A   *Could you come in at 2:30?*
B   *OK.*
A   *It was Mrs. Lee, wasn't it? I'll put you down for 2:30 on Saturday then?*

B   *OK. Thanks.*

A   *OK, Mrs. Lee. Good-bye.*

B   *Bye.*

The students then put the paper away and attempt to recreate a similar conversation from memory. They can fall back on the paper for help if they need it.

Level 3: With the original dialogue to fall back on for help if necessary, the pairs roleplay a telephone call to a garage to fix an appointment for car service.

Level 4: One student in a pair is given a page of a diary with a number of appointments blocked in. The other is given a sheet from the hairdresser's appointment book. They roleplay the call, negotiating to reach a mutually acceptable time for the appointment.

Interviews

Pairs of equal ability can usefully be assigned to interview each other and record the answers. This can be a simple recording of personal information, with questions regarding place of birth, languages spoken, etc., thus providing practice with the kind of questions learners might face in the employment situation. Alternatively, the interview might relate to a theme of study. A unit on the post office might have students asking each other about the frequency with which they use post office services, the postal system in their native country, or their views on the ways in which postal service could be improved in this country.

Completing a form is generally the best way to set up this task, as the format allows for a wider range of abilities. Literacy-level students will find the reading demands easier with a form, and those with low oral skills will be able to make questions merely by reading the box labels with rising intonation, as in "Address?" More advanced students will normally make the effort to turn the minimal box label into a proper question, as in "What's your address?"

Rather than creating different interview forms for different levels of ability, you could create forms in two or three parts, and request students to complete as many parts as they have time for, or as many as you feel are appropriate. Thus all class members will have worked on some section of the task and can review it together. Part one might include the common personal information that all students will need practice at presenting, plus one or two simple questions on the major topic of the interview. Later parts can focus in on the theme, with the second section being factual and answerable with single words or phrases, while the third section asks for ideas, opinions, and experiences, producing more of a journalistic interview.

Other activities for equal-ability pairs

Almost any activity that a student can attempt alone can be usefully done with a partner of more or less equal ability. Pair work allows students to work at their own pace but provides the obligation to perform. It is thus excellent for those students who are inclined to give up on tasks that seem at all challenging. Students can work together on comprehension questions, on writing a letter, on identifying errors, and so on. Working in this way will help students feel at home in a multilevel class and will provide the opportunity for natural, meaning-based communication.

Cross-ability pairs

Although equal-ability pairs work well for students, they do not solve the teacher's problem of trying to prepare materials suitable for students at different levels. However, a number of activities for pairs puts a greater demand on one student than the other. These can be attempted by the majority of learners if the pairs are arranged so that a stronger student is matched with a weaker one.

CROSS ABILITY PAIRS

Transcriptions

More advanced students can act as scribes for those who do not have literacy skills. Ideally this would take the form of a language experience story, with the weaker student attempting to verbalize a personal experience, which is then written down (exactly as said) by the stronger student and later read back by both students together. Some stronger students will want to change or correct what is dictated to them; it should be made clear that this original copy is not for their use but for that of the beginning student. Later the stronger student can make a corrected copy of the story for his or her own records, changing the story into the third person if preferred. The beginner student may also wish to copy out the story or may prefer to work with the transcript version.

The more advanced partners should be briefed before beginning this task so that they appreciate that they are not helping the lower-level students by putting words into their mouths or by correcting them too much. In order to ensure that at least the content of the story genuinely comes from the lower-level student, it may be necessary to assign topics such as "My first job," "What I did over the weekend," "My family," etc. Alternatively, if all the students have at least minimal oral ability, the lower-level students can be told a story that they must then retell to the more advanced students for transcribing.

Not all transcribing needs to be as formal as this. Students might dictate a daily journal or captions for photos selected from piles cut out from magazines. It is important that this dictated material become the property of the lower-level student, as it will then provide for future reading activity. Knowing that the other student will be working from it in the future encourages the transcriber to write neatly and carefully and provide a suitable model for copying.

Interviews

As suggested for equal-ability pairs, interviewing other students and recording the answers makes for useful communication and practices all four major skill areas. An interview process that goes in only one direction can be performed with students of very different ability, with the weaker student being the interviewee. The onus is thus on the stronger student not merely to record answers but to find a way to phrase questions so that the weaker partner can understand

and respond. The weaker the partner, the more challenging the task for the other student. The strongest student can thus be paired with the weakest.

Puzzles and games

The puzzle described under equal-ability pairs, in which one student arranges a set of puzzle pieces into a pattern and then gives the partner verbal instructions for a similar arrangement, is also possible with cross-ability pairs. Instead of the students taking turns, the stronger student always does the instructing. Rather than working on a simple matrix of four or six pieces with another beginning student, learners might enjoy the challenge of working to create a larger puzzle if a stronger student has the responsibility of explaining what is required. The stronger student has the burden of doing all the verbalizing, while the other learner can rely on receptive skills. Once again the demands on the active partner are in proportion to the weakness of the other learner. The lowest-level student can thus be a challenging partner for the most advanced.

Students with a similar spread of abilities can play a version of Twenty Questions in which the weaker partner chooses to represent a person or thing. (A set of cards with ideas can be provided for beginning students if necessary). The stronger partner must find out who or what has been chosen by asking a maximum of twenty questions. Only questions that can be answered by yes or no may be asked, so the demands on the beginner are fairly light, while the other student must struggle to find ways to express questions that can be understood.

Information gaps

Information-gap exercises also can be adapted to students of unequal ability. One student is given an extremely simple text of perhaps four or five lines. The other student is given a much more challenging text. It may be more difficult in terms of language, as in a piece written in technical language or one from an academic textbook. It may be simply a longer text, perhaps an article from a magazine or even a whole resource such as the Yellow Pages telephone directory, with certain pages flagged to show where information is missing. The degree of difficulty can also be manipulated by arranging the order in which questions will be asked. The first question

ROLL PLAYERS

that the strong student will ask of the weak student should be answered by the first sentence of the easy passage. The first question
in the easy passage might be answered by the final paragraph of the
difficult text, thus demanding a search of the whole text.

Roleplays
The essence of roleplay is to give the students the opportunity to
try out the language that they may need to cope with situations in
which they will be called on to speak English. Such situations normally involve interacting with a native speaker, and one of the problems of doing roleplays is that one student must take the role of the
native speaker, a role that should be marked by command not merely of fluency and accuracy but also of appropriateness. In a mixed-
level class, roleplays can be much more realistic when advanced
students take the roles of the native speakers and are responsible
for the overall progress of the conversation. Beginners benefit too,
as instead of practicing only with partners of equal ability, who will

rarely challenge their powers of comprehension, they are given practice in coping with the unexpected and are given a chance to develop strategies for asking for repetition or paraphrase.

Other activities for cross-ability pairs

Advanced students can occasionally substitute for the teacher and provide individual attention for weak students. Some of these tasks will provide useful experience for the advanced students as well. Reading aloud while the beginners follow or merely listen, providing transcription services, explaining government forms and so on can provide a challenge for the advanced student. It is also useful to reverse roles and find some tasks that put the beginner student in charge. Beginners could, for instance, be given a set of word cards that the stronger student has to spell or a set of definitions for which the stronger student must supply the word.

8
Individual Self-Access Material

The next time you are in a bus station or subway and see a bag lady sprawled across a bench, look a little closer at the contents of her bags before you offer her a transit token. You just might see *A Teacher's Guide to ESL* poking out of the top of that bag!

Individual Self-Access Material

The ideas in this chapter are terrific for the students; they offer all sorts of interesting ways to approach ESL, and allow the students to learn in their preferred way and at their own pace. Unfortunately, these ideas also call for a ton of supplies and equipment. Teachers lucky enough to have their own classroom are fine here. Even those who are allowed access to a decent lockable cupboard in the school building will do all right. But those teachers who teach in a church basement, a library corner or a factory cafeteria are not so fortunate. They must lug all their supplies in every day, and they come to feel more and more like bag ladies (or men) in the process. For those who are prepared to carry even more than they do already, or for those who are finally going to demand access to a cupboard on site, the self-access classroom can be the answer to many of the problems of teaching a multilevel class.

A self-access classroom for adult ESL is not so different from the activity-center approach that you may have seen in a local grade school. The teacher provides as wide a variety of activities as possible, and the students select those that they feel are useful and relevant. The activities offered should provide practice in all the skill areas. Each task is set up so that it can be tackled without explanation from the teacher. It has clear directions and provides answers to any questions (on the back) so that the students can monitor their own progress. Some of the tasks will be extremely easy; some of the tasks will be extremely difficult. Students may attempt to read a sentence, a letter, or a short story. They may write a postcard, a diary, or an essay. They are free to select activities at the level they want and to spend as long on each activity as they want. They can work on a task together if they wish, or they can operate as individuals. They take full responsibility for their own learning and select for themselves the content, the style, and the method by which they want to learn.

The teacher is available to those students who need help. With a small group, this can be done on a roving basis: the teacher walks around the class checking on progress and being available for consultation. In a larger group, the teacher may prefer to stay in one place and let students come up when they have a problem. To avoid lineups at the teacher's desk, students can be asked to add their name to a piece of paper and be called when their name reaches the top of the list. If the class has a large number of literacy students, the teacher may prefer to ask the other students to save their problems and use this time to work intensively on literacy skills with those who need it most. Some of the most advanced students could take it in turn to be the class tutor, available for the period to help the others with any problems they have. So long as this kind of tutorial demand does not happen too often, advanced students are generally flattered to be asked and only too happy to cooperate.

Setting up a self-access classroom

In its ideal form, a classroom with self-access materials would have a number of activity centers set out on tables around the walls. One table might hold a box full of reading assignments, arranged in order of difficulty with color coding to indicate level. A selection of unguided reading materials would also be available for browsing, with a newspaper, some magazines, and a small library of books of all sorts—paperback novels, ESL readers, simplified stories, comic books, recipe books, horoscopes, etc. Other tables would hold listening, writing, speech, pronunciation, and numerical centers. Games and other tasks that practice more than one skill would be grouped together. A truly ideal center might even have a video machine or a computer.

Students arrive and, after greeting the teacher and other students, take a master sheet on which they will record the code number of any activities they do that day. This allows the teacher to check on both the students and the materials. The sheets for each student will be kept in a folder and will provide a record of activity over a long period of time, thus helping the student with self-assessment and giving the teacher an overview to ensure that no critical skills are being neglected. Development of new materials will also be affected by the information coming back on their use. If certain activities are proving very popular, it might indicate a need for more material in the same line. If certain types of activity are never used, the teacher will want to look at them again to see whether the problem lies in their level, content, or method. If this were a truly ideal class, no doubt this data would be stored in the computer by one of the students, ready for a quick printout whenever the teacher wanted to review progress.

The reality is likely to be less impressive. Very few of us have a classroom that can afford to give up four or five tables for the arrangement of material, never mind such luxuries as expensive equipment. Self-access is likely to be only one component of our program rather than the mainstay. A good self-access center is not created over night. Rather it is the gradual collection of items of interest and the result of the triumph of the pack-rat instinct. We don't need to wait until we have a perfect center before we can use it. The bag-lady teacher can achieve great things with a single bag of stuff that is dumped on the table for the students to select an activity that appeals to them. Many a teacher starts a self-access center just by clearing out files of years of leftover copies of exercises.

Using the center

Self-access materials put the responsibility for learning squarely on the student. Some learners may take a little while to settle down to this. They may spend inordinate amounts of time making a selection, or they may choose activities that are obviously unsuitable in terms of level. Many of these problems will sort themselves out quickly when students discover that the teacher is not going to tell them exactly what to do. The majority of students choose very suitable materials. Tasks that are too easy may result in the satisfaction of a row of checkmarks, but they have little challenge and soon get boring. On the other hand few students have the temperament to struggle regularly with material that is far too difficult for them.

A more likely problem is that a student focuses strongly on writing skills, for instance, and does not recognize that his or her pronunciation may be badly in need of work. In this situation the teacher and student together can plan out a scheme for future activities. As was discussed in the chapter on evaluation, if students are involved in self-assessment, they will be in a better position to make choices.

Self-access centers can be used with any group of adults, although those who have never before taken responsibility for their own learning will need to be eased into the process. This can often be done by beginning with a simple choice between two activities and building up from there. Such students will at first find it difficult to make their choices and may spend an inordinate amount of time staring at different exercises and trying to decide. Although they are in fact getting good language practice by reading the exercises, they are also likely to be getting frustrated. The teacher might want to intervene after five or six minutes with a suggestion regarding a couple of potentially helpful activities. Students unused to this system will often watch what others of similar ability are doing and wait for them to finish so they can attempt the same activity. The teacher should therefore try to suggest as wide a range of exercises as possible.

The amount of time spent on self-access material will vary with the program. Some classrooms run on a self-access system throughout the course with no teacher-directed teaching at all. Others nominate one class per week or forty minutes per day for this type of work. The length of time will depend on the amount and quality of material available as well as the interest of the students.

Gathering materials

The classroom is arranged into various activity areas, with subjects such as reading, listening, writing, speaking, pronunciation, grammar, and vocabulary, with perhaps even a computer in the corner. Each area ideally contains numerous tasks for each skill level, allowing students the opportunity to find activities that suit both their ability and interest.

Reading

The minimum material is a series of reading passages of all types. Simply for the sake of order it is useful if the texts are mounted or put in file folders so that the individual pieces of paper don't get lost in a box. Each passage is accompanied by a few questions to which the answers are provided in a key on the back of the page. Although all the questions will check comprehension in one form or another, they should not be restricted to simple factual recall. Questions can also be asked on style, mood, vocabulary, inference, detail, and main idea.

The texts themselves should provide as wide a range of reading material as can be found. A typical box might include these items:
- utility bills
- parking tickets
- deposit and withdrawal slips, credit slips, bank statements
- advertising fliers
- completed postcards and greeting cards
- junk mail

- business letters (typed)
- semi-personal letters (handwritten), e.g., notes to school

- completed forms (job applications, credit applications, tax forms)
- recipes
- school report cards
- personnel evaluations
- instructions
- maps and directions
- comic strips with balloon dialogue
- letters to newspaper and lonely-hearts columns
- newspaper articles
- magazine articles
- short stories

The range of material provided must be wide enough to allow all the students to have a chance of doing something. For most classes the simplest level of task would be a minimal text with the format giving a considerable amount of clues about the content. For example, it might consist of a completed check with two or three yes/no questions along these lines:

This check is for $34.00.   YES/NO

The date on this check is March 9, 1986   YES/NO

If the class includes students who are totally illiterate, however, it will be necessary to include preliteracy and basic literacy tasks. The problem here is that although the students might be able to perform the exercise, they are unlikely to be able to read the instructions. If the students have done similar exercises in class and are merely attempting this work for further practice, the problem of directions is less important, but care should be taken to provide an example rather than relying on written instructions. A preliteracy exercise on letter discrimination might be set out like this, with the example demonstrating the meaning of the instruction:

CIRCLE THE SAME LETTER

A		V	A	N	V	Y
B		P	R	P	B	R
C		C	O	G	O	Q

Other ways of making the passages more accessible to literacy-level students include the use of illustration and the use of material that has a distinctive format, such as a bill. For this reason it is best to use original material when possible rather than retyping the material onto a clean sheet of paper.

In addition to a box of reading tasks, the teacher might wish to build up a small reading library. This can include material published specifically for ESL students, such as readers in simplified language, but should also include any material that might catch the students' interest. Secondhand paperbacks acquired cheaply at garage sales are always useful, but often the best success is with illustrated material geared to a specific interest, such as magazines on rock music, gourmet cuisine, sports, fashion, or motorcycle maintenance.

Students who are capable of extensive reading might wish to keep a journal in which they record what they have read, together with their comments. They may wish to write brief commentaries that can be pinned up on a bulletin board or attached to the front of the box of reading materials for the interest of other students.

Listening[1]

At least one tape recorder must be provided, preferably with ear-phones so that the noise does not disturb other students too much. The accompanying tapes should offer as wide a range as possible. They might include the following:

- spontaneous natural conversation, complete with hesitations, overlaps, and incompleted sentences
- semi-rehearsed conversation recorded specifically for the classroom
- scripted dialogues
- radio broadcasts of news items, weather reports, talk shows, and telephone hot lines
- songs to be used with a cloze version of the lyrics (transcript in which certain words are deleted)
- word lists for dictation practice
- letter lists for dictation practice
- telephone conversations
- recorded messages from individual telephone answering machines and from commercial businesses such as airlines
- people talking about themselves

Listening material is more flexible than written material, and you will probably find that you can prepare tasks at many levels to accompany the same piece of tape. A short telephone conversation could be accompanied by a number of work sheets:

- Simple factual yes/no comprehension questions.
- Questions that demand recognition of the mood, relationship, and sincerity of the speakers and that ask the listener to go beyond the words provided to recognize the underlying assertions.
- A memo pad on which the listener writes the message left during the call.
- A cloze exercise. (The choice of deleted words will affect the level of difficulty. Function words are harder to replace than content words.)

---

1. A thorough discussion of self-access listening material is provided in J. Morley, "Listening Comprehension: Student Controlled Modules for Self-access Self Study," *TESOL Newsletter* 19 (1985): 6.

- Completion of a summary of the conversation, demanding rephrasing.

Writing

The easiest way to provide a wide variety of writing exercises without falling foul of the copyright laws is to create them all yourself. Failing that, you can rip a textbook apart, laminate its pages and provide washable felt-tip markers. Learners can then write directly on a page and wipe it clean after they have checked the answers. Textbook exercises have the advantage that they provide an explanation of the task and often answers too, requiring very little on the part of the teacher, but they should be supplemented by writing tasks that are nearer to real life.

Completing forms is one of the most common writing tasks, and the writing center should contain a wide selection for student practice. As well as lengthy forms for such purposes as job and credit applications, work with short forms like banking slips, post office customs declarations, and the back of parking tickets can be helpful. The long forms can also be offered in simpler versions if photocopies are made of only the first section, which normally focuses on personal data. Students may be asked to complete such forms with their own data or to complete the form using data pulled from another source.

Many of the items in the writing center can provide a number of tasks at different levels. Lower-level students might be told to write a check in payment of a bill, while more advanced students are instructed to write a letter complaining that the same bill is incorrect.

Classes held in a workplace situation might want practice with some of the written demands related to the job. Completion of accident or quality-control reports, vacation claims, or other similar material might be useful. A selection of such forms should be available from the personnel office of the workplace.

Some of the tasks should ask students to use their writing skills more creatively. Proper notepaper and photocopies of blank greeting cards, postcards, and airmail letter forms provide a useful context. The accompanying instructions might ask the student to select a card appropriate for a business colleague and inscribe it suitably or to write a note regarding a child's absence from school. Pictures, comic strips, and photographs can be provided to stimulate free writing. Suggestions for vocabulary can be provided on the back of the visual source for students to refer to if they wish.

Students who feel that accuracy is important in their written work may want activities related to spelling. A number of teachers provide small address books for students to use to create their own spelling dictionaries. Rather than making long lists of words to which they are unlikely to refer, students should be encouraged to keep their dictionaries for words with which they have had trouble and anticipate using again. Students may wish to use some of the self-access time to work on the dictionary, testing their own performance or adding new words from the previous week's writing.

Other activities that focus less explicitly on spelling but that still provide good practice are word searches and crossword puzzles.[2] Word searches can be adapted for different levels: beginners are given a list of words to be identified, intermediates are given clues, and advanced students are simply told the number of hidden words and the topic.

Speaking

An individual student cannot usefully do a great deal in this area, so most of the activities are designed for pairs of students working together. Many of the ideas suggested in Chapter 7 are quite suitable for inclusion in a speech center, particularly some of the games, information-gap exercises, and matrix puzzles.

Cards with descriptions of situations to roleplay can also be provided. For low to intermediate students, cards might simply read, "Call the bus company and find out the time of the last bus." Cards for advanced students can be made more challenging by building in mood or relationship and by providing cards for each player so that each has some information unknown to the other. For example, Card A might read, "You have promised to pick up your child after sports practice and now your car won't start. You are really worried about leaving your child alone on the street waiting for you. Ask your neighbor if you can borrow his or her car." Card B might read,

2. A range of crossword puzzles for ESL learners is provided in the four volumes (Introductory, Elementary, Intermediate, and Advanced) of the following series, which make use of illustration as well as verbal clues: J. Crowther, *Crosswords for Learners of English as a Foreign Language* (Tokyo: Oxford University Press, 1980).

"Your neighbor calls to ask about borrowing your car. You like your neighbor and don't want to be unfriendly, but you don't trust his or her driving." If a tape recorder is available, the students should be encouraged to record their oral interactions and listen to their work. They will often be extremely critical of their own performance and spot many errors that go unnoticed in the flow of speech, when they are concentrating on fluency, not accuracy.

For students at the lowest level, speech practice is best tied to listening practice. Have tapes that ask for repetition or tapes that provide one side of a dialogue that students can attempt to complete.

Pronunciation
Pronunciation can be made part of the speech or listening centers, or can stand alone, whichever you prefer. Discrimination drills lend themselves well to this sort of unsupervised work, and students often enjoy the chance to play a drill over a number of times until they

get a perfect score. Self-access work is not so effective, however, in telling learners whether or not an acceptable pronunciation has been achieved. Often one of the roots of pronunciation problems is failure to hear a sound correctly, which means that the students may be incapable of judging whether their pronunciation has improved. Imitation work, in which a student simply mimics sounds heard on a tape, can sometimes be useful for stress, pitch, and intonation, especially if the teacher is able to record the student's own words for repeated playback.

Grammar and vocabulary

Exercises from textbooks are the simplest way to provide a wide range of structure and vocabulary activities. Make sure that any grammatical exercises have the relevant rule explained or demonstrated at the top of the exercise. Choose vocabulary activities of the kind in which the word and definition must be matched, rather than those that may demand knowledge of words unknown to a student who has not worked through previous chapters of the text. A good dictionary should also be available, preferably one designed for second-language learners that provides sample contexts for words.

Computer

A surprising number of schools have a computer sitting around that is already outdated or that nobody ever learned to use properly. If this is the case in your situation, do your best to drag the machine into your class, even if you have never touched one yourself before. Your students will soon sort out how to use it if you let them go at it. Let them teach you how to use it and let them teach each other.

Language-learning software is still in its infancy, and much of it provides only the kind of drill and practice that is easily put on a ditto. Vocabulary, spelling, and grammar lend themselves to this kind of testing, and you will find a lot of software of that type available. It may seem highly unappealing to teachers, but this kind of material is surprisingly popular with students, particularly with those who wouldn't dream of doing the same exercise if it were presented on paper. The novelty of the machine accounts for some of this interest, but another factor is that a machine is nonthreatening. There is no need for embarrassment if failure is known only to the machine, and many students really enjoy the chance to keep trying a task over and over until they are satisfied with their score. This does not, however, justify allowing a student to spend long hours doing an activity which you would hesitate to give out on paper and which essentially is of doubtful value. One way in which software of this type can be made more useful is if students are encouraged to work at least in pairs on the machine, so that they are forced into oral interaction with each other as well as into a written interaction with the screen. This will add a communicative element to all programs but is particularly useful with more rigid programs that focus tightly on grammar or vocabulary.

The kind of programs described above try to take the place of a teacher in that they aim actually to teach the student about language. Some of the most useful software wasn't developed for language classes at all, however, but was designed for business or simply for entertainment. Entertainment programs that work well with language learners include the adventure and simulation games. In these the player is presented with a situation such as being lost on a desert island, trying to solve a murder, or flying a plane. The events of the game unfold in reaction to the decisions made by the player. In a flying simulation, the event may be the crash of the airplane. In a fantasy adventure, the player might only escape death by finding a hidden potion. Such programs present a series of small problems, each of which must be solved if the player hopes for a successful outcome to the game. When such games are played by two or three students simultaneously, the constant presentation of problems can lead to very rich communication as the learners try to assess the most successful courses of action. Most of the games currently on the market make fairly heavy demands on the students' language abilities, as they are designed for native speakers, so they are more suitable for use with advanced students or with groups of mixed ability.

Some of the material designed for businesses is well suited for classroom use, particularly word-processing programs. Most computers have some type of word-processing package provided with them. The simplest word processors work essentially like typewriters, but allow you to go back over your work, correcting any typing errors, adding extra letters, words, or phrases, and deleting anything that is not required. Better word-processing packages allow you to move pieces of text within the passage, to vary the page layout, and to change the size and style of the printing. Some programs will check your spelling, or will search the text to find particular words and phrases and substitute other text if desired. These features are nice to have, but they tend to be more important to a good writer than to a novice. The novice wants a way to produce a good clean copy of a piece of writing without having to recopy the entire draft whenever a mistake is discovered. Generally, text changes made by novices are restricted to adding or deleting information rather than to reorganizing the material in a major way. Even the simplest, most old-fashioned word processor allows that kind of editing. In addition, a piece of writing can be stored in many versions, allowing the student to make comparisons and add second thoughts if necessary.

SHAKESPEARE'S WORD PROCESSOR.

Although literacy-level students may need extra attention when they are first introduced to a computer, a word processor can be very useful, as it relieves them of the stress of letter formation and the concern about getting every letter right. Many beginning adult writers do not like to produce messy work that looks childish to them. They are therefore reluctant to write until they are sure of exactly what they want to say and how it should be phrased and spelled. A word processor gives them a chance to approach writing with less strain and with a little more spontaneity. Initially such students approach the machine best with a computer-literate student, who can handle the programming commands. The literacy student can enter the required text, then give directions to the other student to make editing changes. The editing commands will soon be learned, and the literacy student can then become a teacher of another student.

Other business software that can be adapted for classroom use includes simple versions of a database system. Here information is stored in a cell system, with each piece of information on a given topic being accessible separately. For instance, you might put your checkbook information in a database system. As well as being able to find out what a particular check was for, you can also ask the computer to organize the information for you in various ways. You could ask for a listing of all the checks written to the supermarket in the last six months to determine what percentage of your income is going to food. You could ask it for all checks over $500 or under $25. You can get total figures for utility bills over the year, or you could get figures from different months to make comparisons. Information access of this type can be good in a classroom. Information either about the students themselves, or about any area of interest, perhaps recipes, might be put on file by those students who show the most interest in using the computer. The entire class may not be interested in entering the information but can quickly learn how to access the information; they can then be set tasks such as finding a dessert recipe that uses eggs and chocolate, or accessing a file on local social facilities to compare entry prices or times.

Almost any software can be adapted in some way to the goal of language learning. Even the programs for producing music or artwork will become communicative opportunities if you ask two or three students to attempt the task together and leave them to discuss the product themselves. Do not restrict your choices to software that is designed specifically for language learning.

9

A Sample Lesson Sequence

The one predictable thing about multilevel classes is that they are all different. Very few have a completely even spread of abilities or backgrounds, and the makeup of the class will be affected by the geographic area, the local working conditions, the proximity of other programs, and a host of other factors peculiar to the class. It is not possible therefore to lay down any perfect teaching method. There are a variety of approaches, all of which have value and all of which develop strategies useful to the students. The teacher must select those methods and approaches that seem particularly suited for the needs of his or her own class.

To illustrate the way in which the various activities can be put to use in the classroom, we shall look at one sample lesson in detail.

Student profile of a sample class

This community class of about sixteen women meets two afternoons a week. More than half the women are Italian, many of whom have lived in the area for twenty years or more. Some have been coming to class for four or five years, others have just begun. Other nationalities represented include Laotian, Iraqi, Chilean, Vietnamese, Peruvian, and Indian.

In addition to the usual spread of abilities, there is a wide variation in this class regarding length of time in this country. Some of the older women have lived here for twenty-five or thirty years and are quite fluent. In contrast, the young Laotian woman and the Iraqi woman arrived within the last twelve months. The women have a wide range of educational backgrounds. The Indian woman attended an English-language high school. Some of the Italians from rural backgrounds attended school only through the elementary grades. Literacy problems can be seen in three of the Italians and in the Iraqi woman, who has no knowledge of the roman alphabet. The Laotian woman was illiterate in English some months ago but has made amazing progress and is now functioning at an intermediate level.

The older members of this class joke that it is their social club, as they have been attending for four or five years and have built up close friendships. They have also got a little lazy and rather passive. As well as some new classmates this year they have got a new teacher, Sharon. Sharon is concerned that all the students should take more responsibility for their own learning and is looking for methods and activities that will encourage this. In particular she is worried that the students have tended to group themselves into the old-timers and the newcomers. The old-timer group incorporates not only all the advanced students but also some women who are of limited ability despite their long attendance at class. These students resist any suggestion that they might find the other group's activities more suitable for their level. Similarly, some of the newcomers have in fact made rapid progress but are reluctant to move out of their friendly group into what they perceive as an old-timers' club. Sharon is thus keen to attempt activities that will allow the class to work together and begin to operate as one group.

Description of a sample lesson

Sharon is working on a theme of health. This is her overall plan for this unit.

Approximate time: Eight 2-hour lessons
Objectives: This unit should increase students' abilities in the following areas:
- Join in general class social conversation at appropriate level
- Express an interest in other students and respond to questions
- Develop vocabulary in the area of health
- Understand the basic principles of health care in this country

- Have the nutritional information necessary for good health
- Improve skills of listening for content information
- Practice reading material that has factual content
- Develop the ability to scan tables and identify the required piece of information
- Develop the ability to work both independently and in groups
- Increase the confidence of basic-level students
- Build a sense of unity in the class

In previous lessons Sharon covered the doctor's office, the pharmacy, and the hospital emergency room. Her most recent lesson focused on nutrition. She did a lot of work on listening, with a tape of two women discussing their slimming diets, for which she had prepared four different work sheets. The other major activity involved scanning nutritional tables on product labels to identify specified information. Because the previous lesson was largely based on receptive skills, and thus had the students working alone or in equal-ability groups much of the time, Sharon has planned this lesson to focus more on productive skills.

In this lesson she is working with a rather unusual topic, osteoporosis. Many of the women in the class are older and coming into the danger zone for this disease, so she knows it will be relevant to them. Also despite the imposing name of the disease, the vocabulary for discussing the topic is relatively simple and relates to everyday terminology for food and health that will be relevant even for the beginner students.

Before the students arrive, she draws an illustration on the blackboard (reproduced on the following page) to provide some concrete illustration of the topic and make sure that even the lowest-level students grasp the general idea.

Once all the students have arrived and had a chance to greet each other, Sharon starts the class with some simple social interaction, asking individual students how they are, discussing the weather, and generally demonstrating small talk. She then turns to the diagram on the board and asks the students what they think it represents, drawing their attention to the relative heights of the mother and daughter. The class finds it difficult to identify the characters, and some argument ensues as to whether two or three generations are represented. Finally they solve the problem by

giving names to the two women represented. This allows Sharon to ask questions about the relative heights: "Who is taller in 1935? Who is taller in 1985?" The women realize the point she is making, and some of the more fluent ones offer comments to the effect that they know older women who are smaller now. Sharon asks them why they think this happens and in very simple terms makes the point that it can be the result of poor nutrition. She draws out from them the knowledge that dairy products can be one major source of calcium, which gives her a lead-in to her first prepared activity, an information questionnaire set out as shown on the following page.

In order to provide a challenge for all students, Sharon has not merely provided extra questions for the advanced students, but also more difficult ones. She has included her own name in the list, so that all the students must also interview her and will complete a sheet herself both as a check on the information gathered and as a way of modeling the correct procedures. She will allow sufficient time for the lowest-level students to gather a complete set of answers to the first question; she expects the information-swapping part of the exercise to take about ten to fifteen minutes. Before the learners begin the exercise, she discusses the questions with the students, using pictures of foods to explain the terms for the beginner group so that everyone is clear about the information required.

The students get up out of their seats and move around the room, questioning each other. One of the advanced students seems reluctant to leave her seat and is waiting for people to come to her,

Name _____

Ask the other students:

1. Do you like milk?
2. Which do you like better, cheese or yogurt?
3. Find out how many servings of dairy foods the other students had yesterday. What type of dairy food was eaten?

	Likes milk?	Cheese or yogurt?	Dairy food yesterday?
Maria			
Yvana			
Sisuvan			
Beatrice			
Mala			
Ida			
Natalia			
Teresa			
Vanda			
Sharon			
Donna			
Nanda			
Emilia			
Norma			
Marta			
Mary			
Vi Chau			

so Sharon makes a point of going over and saying, "Come on, Donna, come with me to ask Sisuvan; you don't have her yet." Once the woman is safely away from her seat and busy questioning someone, the teacher leaves her to it and checks on the progress of the lower-level students. Although so many of the class speak Italian, they are making a real effort to ask the questions in English, and seem to be enjoying this chance to get out of their seats and

151

move around. The lower-level students are taking great care to ask the full question "Do you like milk?" exactly as presented on the sheet, while the more fluent students are abbreviating and changing the phrase, "Hey, Vanda, you like milk, don't you? How about you, Maria?" The later questions on the sheet will prove more challenging to them, especially number 3, for which they must produce the direct question form themselves.

The class continues with this exercise for a few more minutes, by which time the more advanced students have all completed the first question and are going on to the later questions. They question each other with very little difficulty but run into problems when they have to ask the same questions of the beginner students. One or two start to use Italian to make their question clear. Although Sharon was happy to let them fall back on their native language in the initial explanation of the task, she intervenes here, pointing out to the advanced students that quite apart from depriving themselves of the necessary practice, they are not giving the beginners a chance to learn. There are a few mutters to the effect that "We tried English; they don't understand," but most of the students acknowledge her point and try to rephrase the question in a way that the newer students can comprehend, breaking it down into a series of miniquestions phrased on the structures used by the beginners. "Yesterday, you eat cheese? Yes? You eat milk? Yes?" This kind of constant drilling provides the beginners with useful input despite its inaccuracies, and they are soon beginning to predict the questions and are answering even those phrased in a more standard fashion.

The beginners themselves are still trying to collect responses to question one. Sharon notices that one woman is making no effort herself but has attached herself to a more fluent speaker and is merely copying down the responses she receives. Once again, the teacher enlists the problem student to accompany her across the room to interview someone else, and prompts her to help get her started. Once she has successfully questioned a few people, Sharon leaves her to it, though keeping an eye out to make sure she doesn't drift back to her friend's side. The student with the greatest difficulty is Beatrice, the Iraqi lady, who cannot read the names on the sheet. She is getting along fairly well by showing the list to people and asking them to point out their name. She cannot read the question on the paper, but she has more or less remembered the phrase "Do you like milk?" although she is still having some difficulty getting it out. What she produces is near enough to be recognizable to the other students, however, and they provide simple yes or no answers for her. Before the exercise began, Sharon wrote the spelling of these words on her paper, and Beatrice laboriously copies them out as appropriate. When the beginners have all completed the first section, Sharon gives the class a one-minute warning before calling everybody together again.

She has drawn a chart up on the board like the one on the interview questionnaire, so that the results can be recorded and compared. She wants everyone to have a chance to write on the board, and to demonstrate their correct results, but she doesn't want to spend too much time on the mechanics of the process. Accordingly, she completes the results for the first student herself, thus demonstrating the form she wants the results to take. She then calls on one of the strongest of the beginning students to complete the results for question one on the first three names on the list, passing the chalk over for the student to write in her results. While these are being written in, an intermediate student is warned that she will be asked to write in the answers for question two on the same three students. This means the second student is ready to start writing as soon as the first student's results are checked. In this way, Sharon avoids the kind of slow results-gathering that makes everyone lose interest.

Once the chart is completed and checked, she asks some simple questions about the information. "How many people like milk? Do more people like cheese or yogurt?" She asks them how much milk, cheese, and other calcium-rich foods they feel they should eat for good health and records their answers next to their actual results for the previous day. Most of the women have eaten well below the recommended minimum, a fact they are to discover in their next activity. She therefore saves this information on the board, saying that they will come back to it later.

Sharon's main thrust for this class is to do some jigsaw work. She feels that it is particularly important that the class should not fragment into the old-timers and the newcomers, and is keen to use approaches that will allow all the students to work together. Although the students have worked with jigsaw methods before, today she is going to try something very new and have each group

153

of students develop materials for the other students.[1] She begins by organizing the class into four groups, based on their literacy abilities.

Each group is given a task, as follows:

Level One: The task for these literacy-level students will be to create a word-search puzzle using vocabulary items provided by Sharon. To introduce the task, she gives them a simple puzzle she has created herself and sets them the task of finding the words while she gets other groups organized. As this group is mostly familiar with the alphabet, she has made the task a little harder by providing the word list in lower case but the puzzle in upper case. Vocabulary for this introductory puzzle comes from the food topic they were working on last week. When she returns five minutes later, the students have all completed the puzzle and are comparing responses. She then gives the group a list of words relating to the osteoporosis issue discussed in the earlier part of the class:

age	cheese	healthy	skeleton
bones	diet	milk	spine
broken	eat	nutrition	tofu
calcium	food	old	yogurt

Their job is to create a word-search puzzle using these words. Sharon knows that this activity will demand close attention to letter shape and to spelling. It will also involve some verbal interaction, as she makes it clear that she wants a joint production from the group, not a series of individual puzzles, thus ensuring negotiation and other communication. She suggests that the group might find it easier to work on the blackboard rather than with paper and pencil and leaves them to it. After four or five false starts, the group opts to move to the board and discovers by trial and error that it is easier to begin with a grid on which the longest word is entered first. Roles soon start to emerge, with one person writing the letters in, another checking their spelling against a master list, and a third searching for new places for outstanding words.

Unfortunately the Iraqi woman is not participating actively. Sharon reminds the group that she would like a true joint effort, but

---

1. This idea was first suggested to me by Sandy Solomon and Sandy Katz of North York Board of Education.

is discouraged to see that when she checks a few minutes later the student is still not working with the group but has begun to attempt a puzzle of her own. Sharon decides that this is obviously a case for compromise and with a mental note to try some activities where the task cannot be performed without input from each student, she leaves them to work things out in their own way. The main group is still busily working on the puzzle when the coffee break comes around, and by this time they are sufficiently intrigued with their task that they opt to keep on going, to end up with the puzzle shown, of which they are very proud.

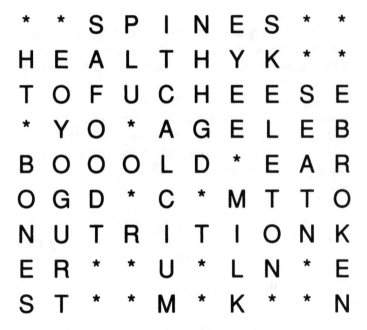

As a final task, the spaces in the puzzle are completed with random letters and the whole thing written on a ditto master so that copies can be made for the whole class.

Level Two: These students are going to make a cloze passage for the others based on a simple text given them by Sharon. Once again she introduces the activity by giving out an example for the students to try for themselves. She has developed a three-paragraph story of a woman describing a fall and subsequent bone damage.

In the first paragraph there are no deletions at all, in order to allow for some understanding of the story on which later predictions can be made. In paragraph two she has removed content words— nouns, verbs and adjectives—which can be guessed at from the sense of the story. In paragraph three she has removed function words, auxiliary verbs, prepositions, and the like, which can only be completed on the basis of grammatical knowledge. She asks the students to complete the cloze individually first, then compare notes with each other about their responses, coming to a decision as to which paragraph they found easiest to complete.

This is the text she gives them:

It was a very cold day, but I had to go to the store. I didn't have any bread. There was ice all over the sidewalk. I walked very slowly. It was really difficult to walk.

I got to the store OK. I bought the _____ and some milk. I came out of the store and _____ across the parking lot. I was carrying the bread and the _____. My arms were full. It was hard to balance. Suddenly my feet slipped on some _____ and I fell down on the ground.

There _____ a terrible pain in my ankle. I tried to get _____ but I couldn't move. A lady came _____ to me and tried _____ help me up. I couldn't get up. She phoned _____ an ambulance. My ankle was broken.

When Sharon checks back on the students a few minutes later, they are arguing the relative merits of their word choices. She points out that a correct answer is one that makes sense and that, for instance, the lady slipped "on the snow" or "on the ice" are both acceptable. She asks the students which part they found easiest, and they all agree that the third paragraph was very difficult. She suggests that they choose "easy" words when they make their cloze for the other students. She gives them a passage to work from, with a couple of guidelines regarding leaving the first paragraph intact, and not taking more than one word out of each sentence.

A Sample Lesson Sequence

While Sharon is checking on the other students, this group begins to discuss which words should be omitted. Some students are in favor of removing the first word they come to, others are more careful in their choice. The product they eventually develop is fairly difficult and has more gaps in it than most teachers would assign. Sharon notes this on her return and demonstrates the problem by removing the original text and asking them to try as a group to complete their own cloze. Despite their familiarity with the text they find it difficult. She suggests that they reserve that version for the most advanced students but provide an easier version by restoring any words they were not able to supply themselves. A third and simplest version will be prepared by listing the omitted words at the bottom of the puzzle. Dittos are then made of all three versions.

Level Three: Sharon has recorded a listening tape for this group. The tape features a doctor talking to a female patient about diet and treatment following a broken hip. The group's task is to develop some comprehension questions on the tape. Ideally, they will work out five very simple yes/no questions, and five harder questions. First they must listen to the tape and agree on the content before they can decide what questions can be asked. They play the tape a number of times and discuss the events described. Sharon has tried to guide their listening by presenting some points to listen for: the relationship of the speakers, the man's occupation, etc. In fact they seem to understand the tape quite well. What they are not clear on is the task they should attempt. They begin to write down answers to the questions Sharon gave them, treating the entire task as a listening comprehension test.

When Sharon checks back with the group later, she realizes that she assumed too much understanding on their part. Never having done an activity like this before, and lacking a clear demonstration of what was required, they fell back on the normal classroom patterns. Although they usually understand Sharon very easily, what she was asking them to do was so unexpected that they all decided they must have misunderstood her, and changed the instructions accordingly. Even when she tries to explain a second time, the group appears baffled. She provides a few sample questions to get them started before she is called away by the fourth-level group who feel they have completed their assignment. When she returns, it is apparent that the help to Level Three was still not enough as these questions too have been answered. As time is running on and the other groups are nearly finished, she finally has to accept that the task was too difficult for the group to do without a much clearer set of instructions and some demonstration. She decides to let them finish their self-imposed comprehension activity and to supply some questions herself to accompany future work on the tape.

Level Four: To this most advanced group she gives a fact sheet on osteoporosis, written by the local health-education authorities. She explains that she needs it rewritten for the beginning students and asks them to pick out the main points and rewrite them in easy language. Later she will ask them to develop some comprehension questions on their adapted passage if time allows. She suggests that the new passage be no more than half a page long and reminds them to use short sentences where possible. The students discuss strategy among themselves and agree to read silently first before getting together to pool ideas. After a few moments' quiet reading, they start to discuss which points should be included. One students assumes their task is to rephrase every sentence and wants to begin with the first paragraph. Another contends that all the important information lies in one section, a list of Dos and Don'ts for good health. The discussion becomes quite lively, with students being forced to negotiate, persuade and present evidence.

When Sharon goes by on her way to another group, she is waylaid to act as referee. Without getting dragged into the specifics of the discussion, she reminds them that the finished product should only be half a page long and asks them to select only the information that is most important. Agreement is soon reached after this, and they start to jot down the points that they feel are critical, arguing now about the phrasing, which forces them to concentrate on accuracy as well as simplicity. They cannot reach agreement about the best form for some of the sentences and resolve the issue by choosing to have each student write out her own version for Sharon to check when she returns.

As it turns out, all the versions contain a fair number of errors. Sharon handles this by selecting correct sentences rather than by correcting inaccurate ones. The correct sentences are then amalgamated into a single entity, and copied out. Having learned her mistake from the already apparent problems of Level Three, Sharon decides to give a very clear demonstration of what is required next and sits down with the group to start them off on the question-making process. Because they have already identified the key points of their text, they find it relatively easy to turn each point into a question, or to restate it for a yes/no response. Once she sees they have grasped what is required, she leaves them to continue alone, which they do without difficulty.

Activities so far have taken about 75 minutes, and the class is overdue for its coffee break. Sharon calls a halt and takes advantage of the break to run off sufficient copies of the dittos for all the students. After the break about half an hour of class time remains. She arranges the students in mixed groups so that each group has one person from each of the equal-ability groups that they were working in before the break. Her aim now is that the new groups should attempt all the exercises developed by the students. Everybody will be responsible for presenting to their new small group the activity that they shared in developing. The lowest-level students start the process, presenting their word search to their new groups. Although they cannot give lengthy explanations, they feel pride in assuming the leadership role and enjoy pointing out words the others haven't spotted. The word search proves surprisingly challenging and even the advanced students occasionally need help.

By the time this activity is done, only a few minutes are left, which Sharon uses for an oral assessment of the day's work. She explains to the class that the cloze and comprehension activities will be done in the same groups in the next class and asks them whether they felt the class was useful. Most of the students have enjoyed the class very much, although there is some grumbling from the group that misunderstood its instructions. Having seen the developments since the break and talked to some of the other students, they realize now what was required and feel a little embarrassed at their failure to produce, particularly as they like to consider themselves among the better students. Sharon reassures them that the instructions were not clear enough, but they still feel unhappy that they will not have an activity to present. She suggests that they each write out a couple of suggested questions at home and come in ten minutes early for the next class in order to coordinate them. The class does not normally do homework, and she suspects that most of them will forget, but they at least have the option of developing an activity if they wish.

159

Sharon's own evaluation of the class is fairly positive. Although there were some problems, these were only to be expected for such a new activity. She was pleased to note that the actual groupings went well, and that everyone now seems happy with the basic idea of jigsaw activities. The extra step of asking them to develop material was a big one and, as with any new method, some time and effort was siphoned off simply in getting used to the new technique. She feels fairly confident, though, that if she tries this again on a future occasion, the students will have a better idea of what she has in mind and will be able to settle to the task more quickly. The class incorporated a variety of language demands with a balance between the oral and print skills, as well as between being active and passive. All students got a chance to develop problem-solving skills and to use their language knowledge to interact.

She decides that in the next-lesson she will keep the students in their cross-ability groups for the other women to present their material, then bring the entire class together again. She has a video on the topic that features two case studies of women with osteoporosis. As some of the medical explanation is too complex for the lower-level students, she is planning to show only one of the case history sections to the whole class, relying on the visual support to carry the meaning. She has developed some fairly challenging comprehension questions that may demand a second viewing before they can be answered; she plans to assign these to the bulk of the class to do in pairs. This will give her some free time to spend with the three students with literacy problems, who are in need of some individual attention that she was not able to give them in today's class.

10
Useful Resources

The following texts are full of good ideas for activities, many of which are suitable or can be adapted for the multilevel classroom.

Bassano, S., and M.A. Christison. 1982. *Drawing out: Second language acquisition through student created images.* Hayward, Calif.: The Alemany Press.

An innovative approach to involving students that can work with all levels.

Dixon, C.N., and D. Nessel. 1983. *Language experience approach to reading (and writing).* Hayward, Calif.: The Alemany Press.

A book on the process of LEA rather than a set of suggested activities, but nonetheless full of ideas.

Klippel, F. 1984. *Keep talking: Communicative fluency activities for language teaching.* Cambridge: Cambridge University Press.

The excellent activity suggestions in this book are grouped by type of activity (e.g., rank ordering, jigsaw, etc.) The aim, level, preparation time, and procedure are clearly spelled out together with any possible variations. The book also provides attractive work sheets where necessary for the activity and gives the teacher permission to copy them.

Macdonald, M., and S. Rogers-Gordon. 1984. *Action plans*. Rowley, Mass.: Newbury House.

All the activities in this book are marked for their intended level of student ability, making it easy for the multilevel teacher to identify those suitable at each level. The activities also have suggestions for related grammar points.

Maley, A., A. Duff, and F. Grellet. 1980. *The mind's eye*. Cambridge: Cambridge University Press.

Fascinating activities based on interpretation.

Maley, A., and A. Duff. 1982. *Drama techniques in language learning*. 2d ed. Cambridge: Cambridge University Press.

The suggested activities are wider in range than some teachers might imagine from the title, and are by no means restricted to roleplay and the like. They include sections on warm-up activities, problem solving, observation, interpretation, and use of literary texts.

Morgan, J., and M. Rinvolucri. 1983. *Once upon a time: Using stories in the language classroom*. Cambridge: Cambridge University Press.

Imaginative ideas for using stories in many different ways, including some that are ideal for the multilevel class.

Steinberg, J. 1983. *Games language people play*. Agincourt, Ont.: Dominie Press.

A wide variety of language games, including many suitable for adults.

Ur, P. 1981. *Discussions that work: task centred fluency practice*. Cambridge: Cambridge University Press.

Ur, P. 1984. *Teaching listening comprehension*. Cambridge: Cambridge University Press.

Both these books by Penny Ur provide an excellent discussion of the theoretical issues behind classroom practice and a wealth of ideas, many of which would work with students of all levels.

Winn-Bell Olsen, J.E. 1977. *Communication starters and other activities for the ESL classroom.* Hayward, Calif.: The Alemany Press.

Although designed primarily for beginner levels, many of the suggestions are suitable for adaptation to multilevel classes. The work sheets (which may be copied) and the section on using pictures lend themselves particularly well to a range of abilities. The book is also full of useful tips from an experienced classroom teacher.

Winn-Bell Olsen, J.E. 1984. *Look again pictures*. Hayward, Calif.: The Alemany Press.

Pairs of pictures that at first glance look identical but actually differ in small ways. Pictures are rich in detail and can be used with any level.

Wright, A., D. Betteridge, and M. Buckby. 1984. *Games for language learning*. Cambridge: Cambridge University Press.

A wide selection of games, each with skill level and related language items identified.

For further reading

Baker, R.E. 1976. "Small group learning." In *An integrative approach to foreign language teaching*, edited by G.A. Jarvis, 37–80. Skokie, Ill.: National Textbook Co.

Bassano, S.K., and M.A. Christison. 1982. Developing successful conversation groups. *TESL Talk*. 13 (3): 18–27.

Bechtold, J. 1975. Small groups in a large classroom. *TESL Talk*. 6 (4): 12–13.

Blair, R.W. 1982. *Innovative approaches to language teaching*. Rowley, Mass.: Newbury House.

Canzano, P.M., and D.M. Canzano. 1974. *A practical guide to multi-level modular ESL*. Portland, Ore.: English Language Services.

Center for Applied Linguistics. 1982. *Teaching ESL in a multilevel classroom*. Washington, D.C: Center for Applied Linguistics.

Courchene, R. 1984. The multi-level classroom or the one room little red schoolhouse revisited. *TESL Canada Journal*. 1 (1): 57–69.

Defoe, T. 1982. "The adult learner, the multilevel classroom and community experience." In *Conference proceedings: TEAL 81/TESL Canada*, edited by K. Waterlow, et al., 105–06. Vancouver, B.C.: TEAL Occasional Papers/Association of B.C. TEAL.

Dubois, B.L. 1979. Localogues for TESOL classes of mixed ability levels. *English Language Teaching Journal.* 33 (2): 106–10.

Elliott-Evans, E., and B.L. Sosna. 1978. "What goes on in a portable multilevel classroom." In *Classroom practices in adult ESL,* edited by D. Ilyin and T. Tragardh, 87–97. Washington, D.C.: TESOL.

Finocchiaro, M. 1978. Teaching learners of various ability levels. *English Language Teaching Journal.* 33 (1): 1–12.

Gibson, R. 1975. The strip story: A catalyst for communication. *TESOL Quarterly.* 9 (2): 149–54.

Helegson, M.E. 1982. Coping with the multilevel classroom: How to modify materials and methods for individualization. *TESOL Newsletter.* 16 (4): 1, 33–35.

House, J., and S. Rooney. 1981. *ESL inservice development program: Teaching a multilevel class.* Victoria, B.C.: Ministry of Education.

Kohn, J.J., and P.G. Vajda. 1975. Peer mediated instruction and small group interaction in the ESL classroom. *TESOL Quarterly.* 9 (4): 379–90.

Sawkins, M. 1978. Small groups in the adult ESL classroom. *TESL Talk.* 9 (4): 29–42.

Smith, R.M. 1981. The ungraded ESL class: Problems and procedures. *TESL Talk.* 12 (4): 27–31.

Strasheim, L. 1979. The issue: Multilevel classes. *Foreign Language Annals.* 12 (5): 423–25.

Taylor, B.P. 1983. Teaching ESL: Incorporating a communicative student-centered component. *TESOL Quarterly.* 17 (1): 69–88.